Whose Learning?

Kate Watson.

Exeter University.

October 2004.

Whose Learning?

Kate Bullock and Felicity Wikeley

Open University Press

Open University Press
McGraw-Hill Education
McGraw-Hill House
Shoppenhangers Road
Maidenhead, Berkshire
England SL6 2QL

email: enquiries@openup.co.uk
world wide web: www.openup.co.uk

and Two Penn Plaza, New York, NY 1012–2289
USA

First Published 2004

A catalogue record of this book is available from the British Library

ISBN 0 335 21407 X (pb)   0 335 21408 8 (hb)

Library of Congress Cataloging-in-Publication Data
CIP data has been applied for

Typeset by BookEns Ltd, Royston, Herts.
Printed and bound in Great Britain by
Bell & Bain Ltd, Glasgow

To
Robin and Mark

Contents

Acknowledgements   viii

1	Knowing how to learn: learning how to know	1
2	Personal tutoring	12
3	Knowing yourself as a learner: the theory	32
4	Helping students to know themselves	43
5	Knowing how to learn: the theory	60
6	Helping students develop skills for learning	76
7	Knowing what to learn: the theory	90
8	Supporting students in knowing what to learn	107
9	Educational relationships	120

References   129

Index   143

Acknowledgements

We would like to thank the numerous colleagues with whom we have developed the ideas that have contributed to this book. David Yates and the team at Cambridgeshire Careers Guidance Limited can lay claim to being its inspiration. They persuaded the (then) Department for Education and Employment that innovative practice such as personal learning planning was worth further exploration and asked us to evaluate their project. We particularly remember the stimulating conversations with Margaret Clements, Sheila Roberts and others on the steering group. We are also grateful to Marion Thomas from Cambridgeshire & Peterborough Connexions for permission to use their most recent personal learning and progress plan.

In developing our ideas we have worked with many schools and colleges in both England and Wales, and we are grateful to them all for making us so welcome. It goes without saying that the real credit goes to the tutors and students who have been so willing to share their experiences with us over the years. Without them there would be no book.

Finally we want to thank Tony Fraser and Andrea Warman who worked with us on the PLP and College Tutorial projects and all our colleagues in the Department of Education at the University of Bath with whom we have collaborated on various projects and who have always been unfailingly stimulating and supportive. We particularly want to thank Dr Elaine S. Freedman for her thorough reading of our final draft, and for teaching us about the use, and misuse, of commas.

1 Knowing how to learn: learning how to know

In schools, much of the learning is managed for students by teachers. However, learning is enhanced if students have a positive disposition towards learning and can manage their own learning, and once they leave school, people have to manage most of their learning for themselves. To do this they must be able to establish goals, to persevere, to monitor their progress, to adjust their learning strategies as necessary and to overcome difficulties in learning.

(Organization for Economic Cooperation and
Development 2001: 99)

Introduction

Whatever your age and experience, learning is a complex process. At school, it can seem stressful, competitive and complicated, and while the anxieties may change as you grow older, indecisions and uncertainties can still blur the best approach to learning. In this book we explore support for learning that seems to benefit many students not only in secondary schools and further education colleges but also in higher education. The book will be of interest to all those concerned with the practice of learning. We think that is everyone. In general, the book is aimed at all those who are supporting learners in formal learning situations. In particular, it recognizes the increasingly important role of the personal tutor in working individually with his or her students, and endeavours to identify and illuminate the processes, professional relationships and learning interactions that underpin this role. In order to understand and apply this practice of learning, we explore the theories, systems, practicalities and tensions relating to it. Drawing on observations from our recent research, we suggest that successful learning is a three-pronged endeavour. Our main assertion is that to understand and feel confident in learning, students need to be helped to recognize the links between:

- their learning of facts, theories and skills;
- their learning of the processes of learning; and
- their learning about themselves as learners.

All these co-evolve and depend on each other for strength and support. If one is reduced, the whole process of learning is likely to be limited.

Increasingly, personal tutoring is being adopted, and specifically customized, by a range of institutions who believe it will establish good habits of learning, both now and in the future. We use the term *personal* to describe learning and tutoring because we believe that while learning is unique for each individual, it is also often a social rather than an individual process. We suggest that the key roles for a personal tutor are largely determined by the triple facets of learning that we have identified. In helping students know what to learn, the tutor's role is that of the expert, who has understanding of the curriculum and experience of the knowledge that needs to be acquired to attain desired goals, and of the different routes towards these goals. In helping students know how to learn, the tutor's role is that of the professional, drawing on training and practice to offer a repertoire of strategies to use in learning. Finally, in helping students to know themselves, the tutor's role is one of supporter and facilitator of the students' own personal goals and reflections. The book aims to identify and explore the theories underpinning this particular model of learning. The practice and philosophy identified can be applied to formally structured classroom learning or to experiential learning in a variety of educational or work locations.

In writing this book, we bring together observations, ideas and theories gleaned from a range of research projects that we have undertaken, together and with other colleagues, over the past ten years. In the text, we have used quotes from these projects to illustrate our points and we indicate the nature of the interviews and the interviewees. These have been at local, national and international level and have involved working with schools, colleges and educators. Our research has, among other things, investigated school improvement, teachers' beliefs and practices, and the actions and reactions of students that lead to learning. We relate our observations of current activities in schools, colleges and classrooms to established theoretical arguments in the hope that this will allow those interested in learning to reflect on and, perhaps, reformulate their own beliefs and practices. The book is structured to facilitate this. Each of the three strands in our model of learning is addressed, first in a theoretical chapter, followed by a practical chapter illustrating some of the ways in which schools and colleges have addressed these issues. In the main, although not exclusively, we draw on activities and policies in the UK as background to our arguments but we believe that the principles and theories that are visited and derived will be of interest to education students and practitioners worldwide.

The current context for learning

We have not yet, nor are ever likely to, celebrate an age when the quality of teaching and learning in our schools is universally praised. Consequently, school-based initiatives for change are driven in one direction or the other by the prevailing political and educational ideologies. They are, almost invariably, fated to revisit and regenerate yesterday's ideas, and then again, move on. For the past 25 years, educational policy has been driven by the insistent requirement for a well educated, highly skilled, yet flexible, work-force (Handy 1997; Brown and Lauder 2001). In parallel, there has been an almost unquestioned call for a higher proportion of students to continue into post-compulsory education (Department for Education and Skills 2002), although there is less consensus about the form and nature of what needs to be learned at this stage (Moore and Young 2001). This conundrum is not confined to the UK. Rationales and strategies for change that focus on personal motivation and targets for lifelong learning; establishing diverse pathways for continuing education; supporting different styles of learning, skills and knowledge (Organization for Economic Cooperation and Development 2001); and promoting continuing professional develop-ment have been observed worldwide.

In the UK, beyond the millennium cusp, much of the dominant dis-course in education is centred around the drive to raise standards in schools and colleges (Levacic and Woods 2002; Woods and Levacic 2002; Gray *et al.* 2003) within the search for a fuller understanding of the processes of learn-ing (Entwistle and Smith 2002) and their relationships with assessment (Murphy 1996). At a policy level, the holy grail of a 'learning' institution or society (MacGilchrist *et al.* 1997; Clarke 2000) is privileged across the globe, although there is much diversity in local practice (Bowl 2002). Unfortunately, as might be anticipated, the current theories do not reliably suggest one direction for change, nor offer clear guidelines for improved learning (students), teaching (teachers) or management (schools). Overall, the signals are confusing.

On the one hand, there are those arguments that are concerned with consistency, measurement and accountability. We feel there is much to commend these principles. In recent years, they have worked to improve provision, foster an equality of provision and monitor the quality of that provision. Individuals and institutions have benefited. However, these policies convey an implicit message to both students and teachers. The message is that learning is mainly a process of completion, determined and directed by the teacher. This may be comforting in its containment, for some students, but it is not the path to independent learning (Lauder *et al.* 1998; Jamieson and Wikeley 1999; Tomlinson and Little 2000).

Knowing what or knowing how?

There have always been dissenters from the well-defined, core curriculum approach and the value of a curriculum that enhances individuality and flexibility has attracted strong advocates (Stenhouse 1975; Handy 1997; Kumar 1997; James and Gipps 1998; Department for Education and Employment 1999). During the 1990s, Brown and Lauder (1992), among others, voiced an international concern that educational systems were not laying the appropriate foundations for a highly skilled, effective workforce. After studying Pacific Rim educational systems, British researchers such as Reynolds (1997) and MacBeath (1997) reported that these countries had begun to value the development of skills associated with creativity, critical thinking and the capacity for lifelong learning, and to place them above the traditionally recognized abilities of recall and understanding.

Meanwhile in the UK, barely ten years after the introduction of the National Curriculum, suggestions that a narrow and constrained curriculum was no longer appropriate were made (Organization for Economic Cooperation and Development 1996; Bentley and Seltzer 1999; Koh 2000). Proponents of this stance take the view that life in the twenty-first century is increasingly complex. In order to cope successfully, young students need to be fully prepared to be a part of what is termed a 'learning society'; to be able to embrace change; to think creatively and interpret evidence in order to solve problems; and to make well-informed decisions. The path to this entitlement (and enlightenment), they suggest, lies in the nurturing of students who are autonomous learners and creative and critical thinkers (Murphy 1996; MacBeath 1997). Furthermore, it has been argued (Sternberg and Lubart 1992) that the main thrust of school education – the imparting of facts and information – is merely the first stage in gaining this entitlement, not the ultimate accomplishment. Crucially, higher-level learners also need to master less concrete and measurable skills such as flexibility, perseverance, self-confidence and social cooperative skills (Claxton 1990; Rogers 1990; Sternberg and Lubart 1992). The imparting of facts and information and the mastery of higher-level skills are likely to complement each other and, in the learning society, need to be interlinked. Those of this persuasion tend to believe that a process of contrived social interactions between the learner and a more informed person allows young people to develop systematic ways of thinking and making sense of information (Wood 1998; Carnell and Lodge 2002).

An issue that was central to one of our research studies (Martin *et al.* 2002) was the tension between the rhetoric for developing creative, independent learners (knowing how) and the reality of constrained teaching approaches that have been shown to ensure good grades (knowing what) in high stakes examinations (such as the General Certificate of Secondary Education (GCSE) taken by almost all 16-year-olds in the UK). There has always been some degree of lip service paid to teaching critical thinking, creativity and independent learning, but appropriate practices have never been long or comfortably embedded in educational institutions in the UK and even less so in other countries. Inexorably, teaching strategies like groupwork and coursework, hailed with enthusiasm at the introduction of the GCSE in 1988 and which possibly might foster independent and creative learning, have diminished in favour of low-risk, routine task completion.

There is a view that personal skills leading to autonomous learning and creativity cannot be taught as a battery of atomistic, technical skills (Lim 1998). The implication is for more task integration and flexibility of teacher support, in order to encourage students to practise different solutions to a learning challenge, and for a variety in styles of assessment to encourage deeper, autonomous learning. Such practices, it is argued, will allow students more opportunity to think for themselves, with thinking in this paradigm implying the higher order skills of selecting, using, analysing and judging information and arguments.

The drawback in this argument is that, over the past 30 years, strategies which have been implemented to encourage individual learning such as child-centred learning, flexible learning and the like, have failed to lead to the promised outcome of visibly improved standards for all. Innovations in the UK (such as the Technical and Vocational Education Initiative, 1991 and the Mini-enterprise in Schools Project (Miller 1993)) have tended to flourish brightly, but briefly, often fuelled by a pot of new initiative funding, but only to fade with its withdrawal. Nor have such strategies always been deemed to be fair and equitable. Invariably, some students require more structured support and frameworking than others, with the inevitable result that particular groups have benefited less overtly than others. These strategies are also vulnerable by being costly in terms of teachers' time and resources, and more demanding and arduous for inexperienced or less enthusiastic practitioners to employ. Hence such efforts have often been derided and abandoned as 'trendy' or 'unsystematic' and have merely resulted in a louder call for 'back to basics' and the generation of more measurable criteria for success. This call cannot, however, be denied. Our research shows unequivocally that outcomes and results *do* matter to teachers, students and their parents, but the tendency has been to argue for results at the expense of creativity. We believe that the two need to work synergetically and argue that personal tutoring can act to support this.

Confident lifelong learners need to understand that learning is a 'process of learning to learn' rather than merely the product of some taught experience. They also need to understand that there is a relationship between the two that is unique to themselves as individuals. Success in the long term is almost certain to require young learners to be widely and fully prepared to be a part of a learning society, able to embrace change, think creatively and interpret evidence in order to allow well-informed decision making. To be lifelong learners or deep learners (as described by Riding and Read 1996) students need to understand the techniques of learning and to be aware of themselves as learners.

The problem is that such outcomes are demanding in terms of equity, institutional time and resources and, fundamentally, teacher skill and commitment. As publicly-funded institutions, schools and colleges have a duty to *all* their students. Like each student, each institution is unique. Individuals, teams, management and leadership all contribute to the strengths, weaknesses and ethos of the whole. All need to be aware of, and responsive to, these areas of strength and weakness. MacGilchrist *et al.* (1997) observed nine intelligences in successful schools. These can be reduced to intelligence about:

- their own systems and contexts;
- learning and teaching approaches; and
- attitudes and relationships.

The school improvement legacy

One important issue consistently emphasized by our own research and supported by others (see Fielding 1997; Joyce *et al.* 1997) is that the student, rather than the institution, should be at the centre of all strategies for school and department improvement. This, we believe, runs counter to the case for a consistent approach to teaching and learning (see Brown *et al.* 1993; Creemers 1994; Reynolds and Farrell 1996). The precept that schools, as well as socioeconomic and home background can and do make a difference to the life chances of their pupils (Sammons and Reynolds 1997) was influential throughout the 1990s and continues to be so. Without doubt, it has raised awareness of good practice in many institutions and the search for the key to *exactly* what it is that makes the difference has been keen. While interesting and important differences in schools and departments have been clearly demonstrated, both quantitatively (Fitz-gibbon 1993; Schagen and Morrison 1999) and qualitatively (Scottish Office Education and Industry Department 1996), the changes in practice resulting from this belief have largely advocated a consistent ethos and systems approach at the institutional level.

Such explorations have sought identification, first, of schools, departments and management teams which are considered to be effective or improving (see Harris *et al*. 1995; Sammons *et al*. 1997; Loyten and de Jong 1998) and, second, of the strategies and procedures by which they operate. The logic is that if schools and departments organize themselves through a system known to be efficient and appropriate, their pupils will ultimately achieve more. This dogma has largely derived from the benchmarking process which is used to improve industrial practice in the field of management (see Riley and Nuttall 1994; Owen and Rogers 1999). Although it has not gone uncontested (Fullan 1993; Elliott 1996) the message, taken up by policymakers, is that successful strategies can seamlessly be shared, transferred and used by less effective institutions, school managers and leaders so that they, in turn, can improve.

Along with others like Entwistle and Smith (2002), we suggest that a major problem with this approach is that it presupposes passive students removed from the core of their own learning. It implies that if the managerial circumstances and environment are correct, the desired learning outcomes will automatically occur. While this, arguably, may be the case in manufacturing, business and commerce, we suggest it is not so in schools where the particular motivation and self-esteem of each individual (and this applies to teachers as well as pupils) are fundamental to achievement at all levels.

While the sharing of good practice between and within institutions is one of the most powerful forms of professional development, consistency is neither possible nor sufficient to promote learning in all situations (Jamieson and Wikeley 2001). Best practice should begin from the needs of the student rather than from the successes of other communities. This argument has moved on from the more non-directive style of student-centred learning which was the *Zeitgeist* of previous decades (see Plowden 1967; Brandes and Ginnis 1986) to the more focused approach of enabling students to understand both the nature of, and the evidence for, their own learning through discussion with, and feedback from, an informed adult (Rogers 1990; James and Gipps 1998).

Whole-class teaching is clearly the most efficient and effective way of imparting defined chunks of information. But it is not enough. Information only becomes knowledge when it is integrated with the consciousness of the individual. This critical step is not necessarily easy. Too often, young people believe that learning can be assimilated without much exertion and they disparage those classmates who demonstrate application as uncool swots. However, there are no quick fixes and students need to know and appreciate the effort that is involved in learning. This requires self-understanding, commitment and flexibility. Learners need to be aware of their own strengths and weaknesses; motivated by their personal short- and long-term aims and targets; and clear about which strategies to select in order to achieve them. Without individual support from a more capable other, not all students will be able to recognize what effort entails.

Moving towards personal learning

The change of emphasis, in some institutions, to supporting learning through the role of the personal tutor has not been a straightforward transformation. Traditionally, teaching in secondary and further education is firmly located in subject areas. Institutions are organized and managed in subject departments. Initial teacher training focuses on subject disciplines, while even in-service training and continuing professional development are strongly influenced by concerns of the curriculum. However, as our society moves towards more non-specific and flexible roles in paid work and in the home, it becomes important for us all to have a more generic view of learning as an adaptable process and an acquired and transferable skill:

> *Student 1:* A subject teacher will help you with the learning of the subject content. They will teach you the course and give you the knowledge based on the area you're studying. I think a tutor is more bridging what you learn in your different subjects together and helping you move on from there into higher education or whatever you want to do.

> *Student 2:* Yeah, I quite agree with that. The tutor can have a bigger role to play – in teaching you how to learn.
>   (Vocational qualification students, further education college)

In pursuit of this goal, tutors need to emphasize the equilibrium between the content, the learning tasks and strategies and the individual learner. As well as understanding subject matter and processes, learners need a very clear understanding of themselves and of others (Brown and Lauder 2001). To realize that understanding, we must first be able to rationalize and articulate our expectations and experiences. Description is needed in order to understand. Understanding is needed in order to develop. As we said earlier, to be competent learners, students must identify their own learning needs and processes and their most favourable route through the learning and life-skill maze. In achieving this and, more importantly, in achieving their desired outcomes, students benefit from the support of a concerned and informed adult. Some students (but not all) will have many adult sources to draw on: parents, relatives and friends willingly provide their own expertise. But it is only the school or college tutor who will have the overview of the student as a learner in relation to other learners of similar age and experience.

Policymakers have not completely ignored these arguments. Throughout the current era of educational reform, an insistent theme has been raising the motivation, self-esteem and empowerment of learners by means of individual guidance for planning and personal control of learning (Department for Education and Skills 2001). The need for investment in human capital to ensure a vibrant and successful society in the twenty-first century has inspired 'think-tanks' like the National Advisory Committee on Creative and Cultural Education (Department for Education and Employment 1999). This group argued that in order to unlock economic prosperity and social cohesion, a national strategy for creative and cultural education is essential. It claimed: 'Creative and cultural education are not subjects in the curriculum, they are general functions of education. Promoting them effectively calls for a systematic strategy: one that addresses the balance of the school curriculum, teaching methods and assessment, how schools connect with other people and resources' (Department for Education and Employment 1999: 7).

Over the years, such concerns have given rise to educational developments such as portfolios and records of achievement (Broadfoot *et al.* 1988; Wildy and Wallace 1998), increased choice through course modularization (McClune 2001), nationally recognized vocational options (Williams 1999; Brown 2001) and more flexible assessment with assessment of prior learning and coursework (Morrison *et al.* 2001; Pope 2001). In particular, arguments for a learning society have supported initiatives such as action planning, individual career planning and personal learning planning (Watts 1992; Bullock and Jamieson 1995; Bullock and Wikeley 1999; Connexions 2001). Personal learning planning supports individual student learning through a process of review and dialogue with personal tutors. In such initiatives, a one-to-one discussion between a student and mentor is used to:

- clarify personal understanding;
- provide impartial information about opportunities and choices;
- establish short- and long-term targets;
- articulate concepts such as transferable or key skills; and
- understand the processes of learning.

The practice of allocating time in schools and colleges for a tutor to sit down with a student (or a small group of students) to review individual strengths, weaknesses and progress and to plan for their future learning is a relatively recent innovation. However, more and more institutions are endeavouring to find the resources to provide this entitlement for their students, especially those that are seeking strategies for improvement (Davies 2001; Martinez 2001a, 2001b). The value of feedback and discussion in supporting learning has become increasingly recognized after work by some persuasive researchers. Thirty years ago, Bruner (1971: 107) contributed to the current debate with his thought that: 'one of the most crucial ways in which a culture provides aid in intellectual growth is through a dialogue between the more experienced and less experienced, providing a means for the internalization of dialogue in thought. The courtesy of dialogue may be the major ingredient in the courtesy of teaching'. The role of the personal tutor is expanding to fill this niche.

Conclusions

For too long, particular philosophies of learning have been seen by their proponents as the sole veridical ontology. Our research leads us to believe that there is truth in most of these philosophies. We go on in succeeding chapters to explore current issues and practice that bring together a range of thinking about learning and the role of the personal tutor. For now we conclude with the three-pronged model of learning in which we identified three main features of learning:

1   *Knowing what to learn* – the importance of identifying the immediate and future purposes of any learning task. This is about familiarity with the substantive content of a course or programme and understanding learning objectives. There is an assessment consideration to knowing what to learn.

2   *Knowing yourself as a learner* – the importance of understanding your preferred mode and route. This is about personal and interpersonal understanding. It is a skill that is required in all stages and modes of learning.

3   *Knowing how to learn* – the importance of understanding techniques for learning. This is about knowing that learning is active rather than passive, but that the same activities are not necessarily equally effective for all learners.

These strands are already addressed by many subject teachers and personal tutors, although in traditional class teaching, the first may be accorded more emphasis than the other two. We suggest that the individual learning discussion can provide equal consideration for all three strands. It personalizes and clarifies learning and has the power to change understanding and attitudes. If dialogue with a personal tutor is to be encountered, in various guises, at all stages of learning and employment, it is vital to understand and establish a good practice from an early stage in schools and colleges. Students need to be clear about why, how and what they are learning. To maximize their power and autonomy, students need to have a realistic overview of their capabilities, capacities and limitations. Many students need help from an appropriate adult to make this explicit and a major role of the tutor is to help students articulate their learning plans and, hence, understand them better. Increasingly, this message is being heard by educational managers and policymakers who place learning at the top of the agenda. Even the British prime minister, Tony Blair, at the 2003 Labour Party Conference, stressed the need for personalized learning: 'Progress in the twenty-first century demands teaching tailored to each child's ability'.

In the next chapter we explore the practice of personal tutoring and how it is being established in schools and colleges.

2   Personal tutoring

*I'll try to encourage the student because if you give someone the
answer they are not going to have ownership of that answer.
Sometimes you have to and say, 'This is what I'd do' but from
discussion we find that the students will find out for themselves.
They'll talk to you and they discover their answers. Obviously
sometimes you have to guide them or push them in certain
directions or if they're missing the point you have to definitely say.
You do give them clear strategies. Being an art teacher I would
never give them my answer because every creative result is
different.*

(Personal tutor, further education college)

Introduction

The ideology of education seems to change with each generation. Before
the 1970s, education was centred round the skills of teachers in imparting
a body of information. Formal and relying on didactic methods, teachers
were seen as the fount of all knowledge (Edwards and Mercer 1987). The
'transmission' or 'traditional' approach was supreme. For the next 20 years
a more progressive, student-centred approach was preached and practised.
Students were expected to be in control of their own learning and to be
motivated by the curiosity to learn. In the UK, concerns with the inconsistencies of this latter approach have resulted, in recent years, in an externally controlled system of education with a prescribed curriculum and high
accountability. Today, a more equitable balance between teacher-led and
learner-led strategies, leading to consistently high standards of quality, is
sought.

Teaching involves helping students to achieve successful learning
outcomes. However, students need to identify their own path through a
particular learning task. This is a constructive process, but the size, shape
and direction of each step is personal for each individual (Entwistle and

Smith 2002). Helping students find their optimal way is the challenge for teachers, lecturers and trainers. Increasingly, educators have been drawn towards a more personalized approach to student support and learning. They believe that having one teacher working with 30 or more students in a classroom situation does not address all facets of learning. Hence, in many schools and colleges, tutor time and resources have been allocated to providing a personal tutorial entitlement for students that includes one-to-one discussions with an informed adult, in a relaxed environment, in order to guide, support and manage individual learning (Bullock and Wikeley 1999; Davies 2001; Martinez 2001b).

Why do we need personal tutors?

Tutors have featured throughout the history of education. Many of the early public schools were founded on a house system with groups of pupils allocated to the charge of a 'housemaster' or tutor for the non-academic aspects of their schooling. A similar pattern developed in higher education, although the Oxford and Cambridge universities' tutorial model is more closely related to progressing academic work.

For much of the twentieth century, in the UK maintained school sector, teaching and tutoring were considered to be complementary aspects of the same job. Up to the 1970s, the tutoring role was, in reality, often limited to administrative contact for a particular age group, class or form, and was largely concerned with passing on information, registering attendance and monitoring. The recognition, during the 1970s (in the wake of the 1963 Newsom Report, the raising of the school leaving age and the establishment of comprehensive education), that teachers should have a care for the personal and social development of their individual students in general, resulted in an expanded role for form tutors. This comprised extended daily tutorial time plus, in some cases, an additional period earmarked for the pastoral care curriculum. This programme of study was determined by the institution and, normally, addressed social skills, behaviour management, health education, careers, subject guidance and the like. Paramount in this pastoral or tutorial role was responsibility for the development of the individual student. Supporting the tutoring role was a pastoral network of year heads and pastoral managers. Despite this emphasis and resource, the pastoral role was often regarded as a remedial safety net and given less priority than academic teaching (McGuiness 1989). We argue that this resulted in the separation of the student as person from the student as learner.

The emergence of critical research into pastoral provision in the 1980s began the argument for the centrality of personal development in the long-term achievement of young people: 'the central purpose of institutionalized pastoral care must be to support the process of learning in schools' (Lang and Marland 1985: 31). Writers such as Lang, Marland and McGuiness believed that the nurturing of affective skills such as social and emotional maturity was as vital to success in later life as the academic achievement in discrete subject areas that was measured by tests and examinations. The role of all teachers, it was stressed, should include helping their students to understand themselves and to support their progress in all aspects of academic, social and emotional development.

These arguments influenced a variety of educational developments set up during the 1980s and 1990s by different funding bodies and agencies. Significantly, these initiatives introduced the strategy of one-to-one discussions between students and a knowledgeable adult. Foremost among them was the Records of Achievement initiative (Broadfoot *et al.* 1988), which was successful in promoting individual reflection on, and recording of, personal achievements. Around the same time, individual career plans, designed by the Careers Service, introduced students to the skills of action planning and making informed decisions (Watts 1992), while the Technical and Vocational Education Initiative (1991) and the Flexible Learning Project (Waterhouse 1990; Tomlinson and Kilmer 1991) emphasized the benefits of individual planning and autonomous learning. All these initiatives stressed the need for students to take control of their own learning, and highlighted the benefits of systems of individual guidance or personal tutorials as effective catalysts in this process.

Reports from Sir Ron Dearing on qualifications for 16–19-year-olds (1996) and careers education and guidance in the curriculum (1995) also emphasized the need for continued investigation into the processes and products that help students plan their learning. In the latter half of the 1990s, the target setting that was fundamental to the government's drive to raise standards in schools complemented these approaches. Guidance on pupil target setting was distributed to all schools in 1998 (Department for Education and Employment 1998). Alongside this, the recent climate of school effectiveness and improvement (e.g. see Hopkins *et al.* 1994; Reynolds *et al.* 1996; Lauder *et al.* 1998) eagerly sought evidence that clarified the impact of particular strategies in raising student motivation and attainment.

From such roots, personal tutoring has developed and adapted to local needs. More recently, the use of personal planning activities has not been confined to schools. Their value has been recommended to further and higher education (Dearing 1997; Carmichael *et al.* 2001; Quality Assurance Agency 2001) as enabling students to understand what and how they are learning and to review, plan and take responsibility for their own learning. Increasingly, the approach has been embraced by employers in the public sector (e.g. the British Army and the National Health Service) and private industry (e.g. the Rover Group, Motorola and the Nationwide Building

Society) as a vehicle for individual development and enhancement. The Investors in People standard (2001), a UK national quality benchmark that articulates good practice for concurrently improving the performance of an organisation and its people, also advocates this approach.

From these beginnings, educators and policymakers began to recognize the benefits of personal tutoring in promoting students' self-awareness, understanding and confidence in their own learning, and in the development of their planning and communication skills. They acted accordingly, and individual tutoring has been incorporated by schools and colleges as a strategy to help raise standards.

Some examples of personal tutoring

Further education colleges

Martinez (2001a) found that, from 80 self-selected 'improving' colleges, over half (58 per cent) had worked on tutoring issues as part of their improvement policy. Indeed, improving the tutorial system was the most widely reported strategy by the participants, and one officially 'improving college' for over five years, cited the decision to introduce a new tutorial system as an important reason for their ability to sustain their achievements. Similarly Davies (2001: 34), comparing colleges in similar areas and with students from similar backgrounds, claimed that tutorials were a very important feature of the institutions which 'make a difference':

> There was widespread recognition of the central contribution that tutorial systems could make to improving and sustaining student retention and achievement. Tutors were seen as a vital personal link with individual students, able to keep a regular check on their academic progress and personal circumstances, and to help ensure that any problems were confronted and dealt with should they arise.

The Welsh Baccalaureate Qualification

The pilot phase of the Welsh Baccalaureate Qualification (WBQ), implemented in 18 Welsh schools and colleges from September 2003, has placed personal tutoring at the centre of this innovative approach. The WBQ is a post-16 curriculum that offers an overarching certificate for qualifications within the UK National Framework for Qualifications at Levels 2 and 3 (QCA 2003). The core of the WBQ broadens optional subject studies by enabling students to study (and gain credit for) complementary topics such as Wales, Europe and the World, work-related and community-centred activities, key skills and personal and social education. Equal value is placed on vocational and academic qualifications, and the framework is structured to make it possible for students to combine and move appropriately between different types of existing qualification (Welsh Joint Education Committee 2002).

The Welsh Joint Education Committee (2002: 5), who were charged with the development and piloting of the qualification, believe that personal tutors are central to the success of the project and are critical in achieving its aims:

> All students will benefit from the guidance and mentoring pro-vided by their personal tutors and careers guidance as an integral part of the curriculum. The core will allow schools and colleges to provide a flexible framework for each student, with the emphasis on time for tutoring and mentoring shifting the focus to the indi-vidual. This will be especially important in improving student retention and achievement.

The Connexions Service

The provision of guidance for course selection and planning for future development and careers is a feature of many countries with a well estab-lished education system. In the UK, independent careers companies, many of which cover specific geographical areas or local education authorities, receive funding from the government to provide careers-related services for individuals, schools, colleges and businesses. In line with the government's strategy, the overall mission of such companies is to provide the most favourable conditions through education, training and work so that every-one can achieve a fulfilling lifestyle and have a stake in society. Ultimately, it is argued, this will make for a more economically competitive society.

As part of this provision, the Connexions Service was set up by the UK government in 2001, as a branch of the Careers Service with a remit to offer a range of guidance and support for 13- to 19-year-olds to help them make a smooth transition to adult life. In line with other careers companies, Connexions provides a network of personal advisers that means students can access a full range of advice and guidance on 'anything stopping you getting on in life', from one person in one place. Help is also available online and over the telephone. Careers advisers are attached to particular schools and colleges and many have designated slots when they are avail-able to advise 16- to 19-year-old students on a one-to-one or whole-class basis. Sessions with a careers adviser will provide valuable information for student decision making and can usefully be included in action planning tasks. They do not however, replace the one-to-one sessions between a student and their personal tutor which explore the processes of decision making for knowing what to learn and knowing how to learn.

As part of the development of this provision, we became involved in an initiative launched in 1995 in a county in the East of England. The initiative was titled 'Personal Learning Planning' (PLP). It was introduced to schools by the local careers guidance company and has informed the development of the Progress File which is now available nationally, and will replace the National Records of Achievement throughout England and Wales by July 2004. The Progress File is a set of guidance and working materials to help young people from age 13 and adults to record, review and present their achievements, set goals and make progression in learning and in work. It will be used voluntarily in schools, colleges and employment, and also by the Connexions Service.

We were the external evaluators for the PLP project and it has provided much material for this book. We do not apologize for this as it was this research that stimulated our own reflection on the tutoring process and its real aims and objectives. A stated aim of this project was to embed good understanding, and habits of, learning which would support students in the latter years of secondary school and into further or higher education and beyond. The specific objectives of PLP were to:

- motivate and increase self-confidence by involving students in planning their own learning and personal development;
- ensure that students regularly reviewed progress and set learning and other targets with tutors; and
- develop communication, negotiation and planning skills in students.

PLP was centred on Year 9 students (13- to 14-year-olds) and was both a process and a product. The process depended on an individual (or sometimes small group) discussion between the student and a tutor. The tutor was usually the class teacher or another teacher who knew the student well and had an overview of his or her progress. The personal discussion focused on evidence about current achievements – in and out of school. It guided reflection on these achievements and identified any uncertainties or problems. Realistic plans for the future were made, and shaped into the pupil's own goals for improvement. The product captured this personal discussion. It was an action plan, normally written by the student, setting out clear personal, educational and vocational goals or targets, together with appropriate actions and deadlines to achieve them.

One group of schools used a common pro forma to help focus the dialogue on the action planning cycle. This was a two-sided, A4-size sheet. It began with a section on *Where am I now?* which covered the students' perceptions of their strengths, weaknesses and achievements. This was followed by *Where do I want to be?*, exploring aspirations and ideas, long and short term, for the future. It concluded with *Setting targets* in three areas: personal development and social life; school activities and work; and beyond school and careers related. A similar format used by Year 9 students in the Cambridgeshire and Peterborough Connexions area in 2003 is shown in Figure 2.1.

PERSONAL LEARNING AND PROGRESS PLAN

connexions

CAMBRIDGESHIRE & PETERBOROUGH

This Plan has been written following discussion with my tutor. It outlines what I have learned about myself and my progress, which has helped me to set my future goals, and my targets to help me achieve them. Further information can be found in my Progress File.

Name   Year Group

School   Date

Personal Statement
Summary of academic and personal achievements, skills, qualities, likes, dislikes, strengths and areas for development.

Goals for Progress
What I want to change, improve and achieve in all areas of my life: in school life, personal life and future life.

Targets for Progress
Action that needs to be taken for things to happen
so that goals can be achieved.

Personal Development Targets
To help make progress and achieve my personal life goals I need to:

_____

_____

_____

_____

School Development Targets
To help make progress and achieve my school life goals I need to:

_____

_____

_____

_____

Career Development Targets
To help make progress and achieve my future life goals I need to:

_____

_____

_____

_____

Follow up
Do I need any more information, advice and guidance now?
If so, where can I find this help?
(e.g. Connexions library, Connexions PA, www.purplepigeon.net, other) _____

_____ When will I review my plans? _____

Student's signature   Teacher's signature

Figure 2.1 *Personal Learning and Progress Plan*

Tutors, students and educational relationships

All our research has indicated that a one-to-one conversation between a student and a personal tutor is successful in that both students and tutors value the discussion, feel that they develop a better relationship and learn about each other. Tutors, teachers and educational managers agree that there is potential benefit for:

- *the student* – through clarifying their own strengths and weaknesses and in making future plans;
- *the tutor* – through improved knowledge and understanding of their students; and
- *the institution* – through identifying success and pre-empting problems.

In the PLP project, it was clear that most teachers were keen to assume the role of the tutor. They felt it was an opportunity to interact with, and learn about, their students at a more informal level. Similarly, students felt encouraged that their tutors had time to sit down and chat with them, individually, about their wider interests. Many came away with the feeling that their tutors genuinely wanted to help them, and for some this was a novel idea (Howieson and Semple 1998). Students had benefited from the opportunity to talk about themselves: what they were good at and what they found difficult. They had also been encouraged to think about strategies for improving their skills in and out of school. When we asked students to look back over PLP with hindsight from Year 11 (at age 15 to 16) they indicated that it was often their first experience of systematically planning their learning, but the realisation of the importance of this only crystallized some time after the event.

There is some evidence to suggest that the process of one-to-one dialogue or small-group discussion which underpins action planning produces more measurable effects with particular groups of young people (Bullock *et al.* 1996), often those most in need of support. PLP was used constructively in both mainstream and special education schools. In special education schools the steps for learning were clearly deconstructed and shared with the student. By contrast, a major finding from the PLP evaluation was that there was little discussion in mainstream schools of how to realize goals and what students precisely needed to do to achieve their targets. Hence, in some mainstream schools, the students were less aware than their special education peers of the relationship between the one-to-one dialogue and subsequent target setting and their practices of learning.

Institutional issues

Evidence from our observations and discussions in schools and colleges leads us to believe that learning institutions will enhance their collective intelligence (MacGilchrist *et al.* 1997) and individual potential by considering issues fundamental to the nature and processes of learning. If a learning innovation like personal tutoring is to be really successful in terms of improved learning, it is not enough to regard the process merely as an informal chat with *ad hoc* follow up. The broader picture of the change, including its rationale and theoretical antecedents, its wider links and its current aims and processes needs to be considered by all those responsible for implementing the system. It is therefore important that this innovation, like all innovations, should be considered within the context of the institution.

Timetabling

The first question to be asked by institutions moving to systems of personal tutorials is, *What can we do with our current capacity and resources?* Practical issues of timetabling need to be tackled by the team with responsibility for curriculum planning. We have observed different styles of personal and group tutorial provision and have encountered creative ways of releasing tutor time for dedicated one-to-one sessions. These include the following.

- Team teaching the tutorial programme so that individual tutors can be released at regular points throughout the academic year for their one-to-one slots. This is perhaps the most feasible and cost effective method, but poses the problem of large groups for some tutorial topics.
- Cover from either internal or external sources to release the tutor at regular points throughout the academic year for one-to-one slots. This works well when time and financial resources allow, although there can be problems finding supply cover in shortage or unusual subject areas.
- Additional one-to-one slots in a tutor's timetable. In these times of financial stringency, not all schools and colleges have the extra capacity for this option.
- Use of activity week. This was successful in schools where one-to-one slots were restricted to particular year groups at a specific time of year.
- Suspending the timetable for a day. The last day of term was used in some colleges for personal tutor sessions. This was thought to be practical when all students in the institution were entitled to one-to-one sessions with their tutor. We found schools who also used

this strategy, but usually only once in the academic year. Sometimes it was called a 'study day' with students working, either supervised on unsupervised, on projects of their choosing until the time of their one-to-one session.

- Establishing posts that are solely tutorial. In one 11–18 college, capable and respected senior members of staff were identified as 'super tutors'. They had no subject responsibilities, but had tutorial responsibilities for all students in the upper level of the school. For this school the tutorial role was seen as vital in ensuring effective learning and informed choices.

We have also observed situations where teachers have been asked to organize one-to-one tutorials in lunch hours and after school. While caring and committed teachers have complied with such requests, inevitably they tend to be resented as additional duties and not integrated into the learning core.

Some tutors suggested that tutorials were more effective at the beginning of the week when plans for the coming week could be discussed, but this seems to be a problem of clarity of purpose rather than of timetabling. However, the timing of tutorials was important to the students and appeared to have an impact on their perceived value. The issue for students was more concerned with the position of the tutorials within the timetabled day. While a gap between tutorial time and subject time could provide useful unsupervised time, and some students said they made good use of such slots, others failed to have the structure or will to do so. All students interviewed in one institution cited examples of classmates who chose to wander into town during unsupervised time between subject and tutorial periods:

Student 1:   I can't be bothered to come anyway.

Interviewer: Because it's after lunch?

Student 1:   Yes. After this lesson we have to wait two hours for 45 minutes and that's what really gets on our nerves.

Student 2:   It's a really long time between this lesson and the next one.
       (Vocational qualification students, further education college)

Characteristics of a good tutor

Among the tutors we have interviewed there was broad agreement about the nature of the role and the characteristics that distinguish a 'good' tutor:

> So the whole discussion has led into what is required to support the learner and one of those is quite clearly the role of the tutor ... we advertised within the college for people to come forward with ideas which would enhance the learner's experience at the college. Two or three of those came forward with ideas about how they could enhance tutorial provision and set themselves up as role models ...We've also had a very good 'blue skies' day where loads of ideas came out and some of the follow up about that was the need to give various support to the learner. We then built on that and put action plans in place for more personal tutorials.
>
> (Deputy principal, further education college)

Most believe that it is essential for staff with a tutoring brief to be fully committed to the task, but nearly all said they knew of colleagues who were not 'on board'. This, it was observed, has a detrimental effect, with students picking up negative feelings about tutorial sessions from the tutor. Both students and teachers identified characteristics of good tutors as:

- empathy with students;
- understanding of students' needs and circumstances; and
- fairness and decisiveness.

The personal characteristics, background knowledge and experience and preferences of the individual tutor need to be recognized, first by the individual themselves, and second by peers and managers. This was seen as important in ensuring that the full range of responsibilities was discharged within the student-tutor relationship.

Others to whom we talked felt equally passionately that personal tutoring required skills and qualities that were not found in every member of staff. These respondents felt that it would be of more benefit for students to receive tutor support from individuals who were more naturally inclined to the interpersonal approaches fundamental in supporting students' learning and well-being. This view implies a larger role for fewer tutors with talent and enthusiasm in this area. Conferring status on such tutors (super tutors?) with the consequent professionalization of the role could be persuasive and is the system currently favoured by many colleges.

Sharing values and practice

Just as important as clear and appropriate systems for delivering personal tutorial entitlements, are shared perceptions and values relating to the role of the tutor and the conduct of the tutorial sessions. Where time was found in meetings or staff development sessions to discuss fundamental issues, schools and colleges noted that greater importance was attached to the tutorial sessions. Some of the questions that have been explored in schools and colleges include the following:

- To what extent should there be consistency of tutorial purpose and provision across a large and diverse institution?
- What criteria should there be for identifying staff as personal tutors?
- How can tutorials be organized most effectively and efficiently?
- What are the professional development implications of personal tutoring?
- What should be the mechanisms for monitoring and evaluating tutorial provision in an institution?

In some larger institutions we have come across clear internal differences in the content and style of tutorial activities (Bullock and Fertig 2003). For example, in colleges with diverse faculties and departments, delivering a range of qualifications and with flexible attendance patterns, different systems often evolve for tutorial provision. In one such college, most tutors claimed to deliver a mixture of whole-group sessions and one-to-one interviews. However, the balance between one-to-one and whole-group activities was largely determined by the perceived needs of the students – from the tutor's own observations or from information from colleagues. It was also fashioned by the tutor's personal views on the aims and objectives of the tutorial programme. As tutors showed disparate understanding of the aims, nature and structure of the tutorial programme, this led to inconsistency of provision. Students experienced a range of formats for their timetabled tutorial slots, which ranged from no structured or organized activities with one-to-one sessions, arranged if and when necessary, to clearly structured activities related to assessed subject work and one-to-one tutorials by rotation with additional one-to-one slots if required. Problems from this diversity were identified as:

- perceptions that the personal tutorial system was not regarded by staff as an integral aspect of the educational experience;
- dissatisfaction that some tutors were entrusted with regular slots for tutorial work but were using this time inappropriately; and

- concern that students were not receiving what was seen as an 'entitlement' to personal tutor support.

While the balance between a consistent approach to student entitlement and staff autonomy needs to be resolved in the best interests of an institution, it is important that a shared view of the nature and purpose of the role of the tutor is developed at the outset of tutorial provision (Martinez 2001a; Green 2002). The benefits of organized staff development seminars and workshops to raise the profile of personal tutoring have been consistently stressed by those with an interest in this form of support and guidance: 'The Personal Tutor will be trained to understand the professional requirements of the role, including the skills to deal with pastoral matters, and will be supported in carrying out these functions' (Welsh Baccalaureate Qualification 2003: 1).

Another dilemma that schools and colleges must confront when setting up their tutorial system is whether to follow the practice of tutors continuing with their tutor groups through successive years or whether tutors should concentrate on a particular key stage. There is a tension here between, in the first instance, encouraging all tutors to become involved in the tutorial process, and allowing students to interact with adults who have come to know them well; or alternatively, encouraging certain tutors to become experts at key stages which might allow a higher quality of advice for students at progression points. It can be argued that if the tutorial model is predicated on fundamental knowledge of the young person, and is about giving reliable feedback to help young people set goals within a framework which allows the tutor to call on other experts, the first option would be more effective. Weaknesses inherent in this model are personality clashes and the need for all tutors to be abreast of current options and policies (see Hodkinson and Sparkes 1993). On the other hand, the second model would allow some selection of tutors with expertise and a particular interest and knowledge of progression at the different stages. In our investigations, no simple answers to this dilemma were apparent and it seems that each institution must consider the options with their own resources of tutors and other professional expertise in mind.

The realities of school and college suggest that while it may be desirable for personal tutors to be selected from those who express an interest or who have some expertise in the area, it is likely that other pressures will prevail. Most staff, regardless of their strengths and weaknesses, will be involved in tutorial responsibilities (see also Bullock and Wikeley 2000; Green 2002). The need to identify a sufficient number of personal tutors from an existing pool of teachers and lecturers can result in limited options.

The need for continuing professional development

There is a need for dedicated induction and professional development in all forms of tutoring for all teachers and lecturers. In one of our research projects (Bullock and Fertig 2003) we found that almost two thirds of staff with responsibilities as tutors had no previous experience of personal tutoring and that only 42 per cent of respondents had any professional development related to their role as a personal tutor (see also Marland and Rogers 1997). There is, clearly, a need to draw on strategies such as mentoring for new personal tutors, modelling of positive personal tutoring, and sharing of techniques for small-group and one-to-one discussions. The comments of Green (2002) in relation to the dearth of skills training for the tutorial role and the planned and structured observation of effective tutorial practice are likely to be of relevance here:

> *Researcher:* Is there any training for the tutorial role?
>
> *Tutor:* I have provided some in faculty and it's alluded to on the teacher training programme, but it's not high priority, no. At the beginning of last year I did some training of personal tutors around discipline procedures and how to run an induction programme and lots of people who'd been tutors for quite a while wanted to come because they hadn't had any training and wanted to make sure they were on the right lines. They felt they were but wanted to make sure.
>
> (Female tutor, further education college)

There has been cautious support in some institutions for a newly-created role of senior tutor, though this has occasionally been leavened by a general lack of awareness of their remit:

> *Tutor:* I also think there should be very clear structures for support along the way. There is in theory, we've got that senior tutor role, but not everybody will know easily how to access that or what is appropriate to use.
>
> (Female tutor, further education college)

Any reservations have focused around the priority senior tutors give to providing direct support for tutors and, additionally, the part played by senior tutors in the monitoring and evaluation of tutorial provision. In one of our surveys (Bullock and Fertig 2003), both questionnaires and interviews indicated that some staff felt there was a need for senior tutors to provide detailed lesson plans and resources that staff could use during timetabled tutorial slots. Other tutors felt happy with the more distant, monitoring role of the senior tutors and were content to make use of them essentially as a fallback position. An opportunity for colleagues to work together to develop a clear, shared understanding of the respective roles and responsibilities of the personal tutor, senior tutor and external agencies was felt to be a priority. This was especially relevant in areas such as the monitoring of attendance, the progress of students within the taught curriculum, and the overall welfare of students.

For personal tutoring to have a real impact on learning, progression and retention it is necessary, first, for both students and tutors to recognize the value of planning and understanding the processes of learning, and second, for the tutor to be the fulcrum of each student's individual strategies for learning. As Gray (1995) stressed, one of the three indicators of an effective school is that each student has a vital relationship with at least one teacher. The role of the personal tutor in helping students develop skills of personal reflection and self-assessment cannot be understated. The recognition of the importance of the personal tutor and clarity of provision for each student is probably more valuable than consistency across an institution.

Establishing student ownership

To be most effective, the authority of the one-to-one tutorial must reside, to as great an extent as possible, with the student. Therefore there is also a need, if they are to fully engage, for the students to go through a process similar to that of staff development. The content of each one-to-one session should be, at least partly, determined by the student him or herself. Our research indicated that it is more natural for older students to assume this responsibility. Younger students, although welcoming the opportunity for an individual discussion with their tutor, tend to see the one-to-one dialogue as a school requirement, often related to making option choices or to setting targets (Bullock and Wikeley 1999). This could be a matter of poor understanding or lack of confidence in the one-to-one interactions. Induction into the purposes and processes of personal tutoring may be required for some students. Induction to the one-to-one tutorial needs to be flexible according to the needs of students and can include the following:

- An introduction to the personal tutor and the group. This can include a sharing of backgrounds, logistical arrangements and information on how to access the tutor and other members of staff.
- Discussion on prior experiences and expectations of the personal tutor system. This can lead to a shared understanding of the aims and purposes of the system and one-to-one tutorials.
- Requirements and ideas for effective individual record keeping. We have found that this is often the least enjoyed aspect of

one-to-one. It is important that students understand the need for clear records and that student preferences in creating these are heard.

- Ice-breaking activities. These are numerous, and usually fun. There are ideas on the web which can be tailored to help students think about their own strengths and needs without making anyone feel uncomfortable.
- Considerations of strategies for effective learning. This could include sharing personal skills for learning, an introduction to the concepts of different learning styles and some reflection on the personal implications of these.
- Explication of criteria for assessment and discussion of what these mean in real terms.

When tutors were asked what should be included in effective one-to-one sessions they suggested:

- preliminary time for the student to reflect on and evaluate their current learning;
- some negotiation of the purpose of the tutorial with the student;
- a celebration of what the student has achieved and an identification of challenges that need to be confronted;
- a recognition of key and transferable skills and a discussion of how the student might use these in a different situation;
- a personal review to prioritize actions and set targets;
- additional time to capture a record of the one-to-one session; and
- an agreement for a firm date when the student will evaluate their intended actions and targets, reflect and make sense of the learning process.

The organization of tutorials varies according to the resources and ethos of individual institutions. Nearly all have some form of whole-class tutorial and (or) pastoral care slots identified in the timetable for all students. The opportunities for one-to-one sessions vary from one a year to one every half term with a tendency for post-16 colleges and larger institutions to support the more frequent meetings. On the other hand, we spoke to some full-time students in colleges who never had a one-to-one discussion with their tutor even in the final weeks of the academic year. Some complacency from tutors was implied here, as tutors stressed that students were able to request a one-to-one discussion if they wanted it, but from the student perspective this was a rare demand.

Students also valued their meetings as a whole tutorial group. There was a feeling that some things were better discussed in groups and, also, that group meetings were good for making friends and providing a social base:

Researcher: Do you talk about the same things in the other interviews as in the one-to-one?

Female 1:   It's not as personal if you're with a group. If you're on your own you can talk about anything.

Female 2:   The questions, but not all the answers, are the same.

Researcher: So you may say some more personal things, but you're still looking at the same sorts of things?

Female 1:   You might have more social goals when you're in a group and more personal when you're on your own.

Researcher: But you might be talking about your learning or targets in either of those interviews.

Female 1:   Yes.

(Year 9 students, comprehensive school)

Again, the structures of the whole-group sessions varied, with students telling of a range of experiences. For some, group tutorial time meant engaging with general issues within a tutorial 'curriculum' devised centrally by the institution. The emphasis in these tutorial sessions was on issues such as careers, drugs education, finance and the like. Others spent their tutorial sessions working on material associated with the courses they were following. A final group of respondents appeared to be largely left to their own devices within the timetabled tutorial meetings.

Group and one-to-one meetings were thought to complement each other and both were felt to be needed by students. The students stressed that the best groups should not be too large, with around 15 to 20 cited as appropriate. In colleges, it was noted by tutors that the size of the tutor group varied greatly between courses and departments and that this could have an impact on the student-tutor relationship. The few students who had no structured activities in their tutorial sessions perceived their group as no more than a forum for receiving notices.

Tutors believed that students (whatever their age or area of study) preferred clear structure. However, all agreed that a good tutorial programme needed to be flexible and adaptable to individual student needs and the various pressures within the academic year. Students also argued that tutorials should have different structures and foci at different times of the year. They suggested a variety in topics covered and a gradation in time allocation and in the balance between group and one-to-one. Students felt that the format of the tutorials needed to be flexible to take account of the differing demands on students through the year:

> Middle of the year need tutorials to sort out work demands. Also at the beginning of the year when you start off doing your course, so you can tell him if you're enjoying the course, if there are bits you're finding difficult, if you find a bit that you don't actually want to be doing. You could actually use that time to sort it out first thing in the year.
>
> (Academic course student, further education college)

Students suggested that an effective tutorial programme might comprise a mixture of:

- large combined groups addressing common interest issues led by an internal or external speaker;
- whole groups working with their tutor to develop a sense of community and general learning and key skills;
- small groups to share common issues, model good learning practice and extend peer support; and
- one-to-one sessions to discuss individual learning approaches, strengths and weaknesses and to set out a future learning plan.

Conclusions

This chapter has outlined the provenance of personal tutoring and has discussed some of the institutional issues that need to be considered. A one-to-one discussion with an informed tutor or mentor can help to focus the effort required to transform whole-class information into personal learning. Skills, strategies and styles for learning can be identified and adopted or adapted for individual use. It can be helpful to identify any issues that are beyond the individual's control and those which can gainfully be manipulated in some way. Decisions that have to be made can be identified, and the information that will inform that decision making gathered. Clear actions can be noted for both the short and long term. A one-to-one discussion between the student and their tutor that articulates and examines the student's own perceptions of successes and weakness, and encompasses individual support and guidance, is a catalyst for the effective learning of both participants. This support provides technical tools such as organizational issues and learning strategies and also psychological tools concerning matters of motivation and behaviour (Daniels 1996).

As Carnell and Lodge (2002) argue, however, too often the rationale and goals of tutoring are not well articulated by those participating in the process. While excellent practice in tutorial programmes, as described by Davies (2001) indubitably exists, practices and cultures in schools and colleges remain diverse and heterogeneous (Simkins and Lumby 2002). An understanding of the role of the personal tutor in the development of students' achievements and learning needs to be fully explicated and shared between those teachers and students involved in the interaction. We argue in the following chapters that this is best done by understanding the three key elements of learning, namely:

- knowing what to learn (Chapters 7 and 8);
- knowing how to learn (Chapters 5 and 6); and
- knowing oneself as learner (Chapters 3 and 4).

It is helping the student to understand the interconnectedness of these three elements, in a range of contexts, that is the major role of the personal tutor. For the purposes of clarity we have separated the three strands in our discussion. In writing this book we had many discussions as to whether or not there was a hierarchy that would help structure the book. For example, is knowing how more important than knowing what? Where does knowing self fit with the other two? We came to the conclusion that it was the inter-relationship that was the important part, and therefore nothing should be assumed from the order of the chapters. Each element is discussed in a pair of chapters. In the first we explore the theoretical support for the importance of the element. In the second we use examples of practice we have observed in schools and colleges that we think raise interesting issues for other practitioners.

3 Knowing yourself as a learner: the theory

Researcher:	*What do you think personal learning plans are for?*
Male 1:	*To find out about ourselves, so we can actually realize ourselves what we want to do and then find out the foundations about how to achieve that.*
Male 2:	*I think personal learning plan means that it's your personal way of what you need to learn and it's your plan for that and what you need to be looking at.*
Female 1:	*There's also things like you as a person, your strengths and weaknesses and how people see you.*

(Year 9 students, comprehensive school)

Introduction

Much is demanded of the educator in the school and in the classroom: a greater emphasis on evidence of cognitive achievements in relation to both schools and students competes with an identified need to nurture social responsibility and emotional maturity in young people. In more and more educational systems, it is becoming generally accepted that education is about developing 'students as life-long, self-regulating learners' (Thomas and McRobbie 1999: 667). This implies helping students towards a sound personal understanding of their individual values, strengths and aspirations and a knowledge of how these interact with development and learning. Embedded within this view is the concept of learner identity. The rhetoric of lifelong learning contains much about the recognition by the individual of him or herself as a learner, in a multitude of contexts. Learning is not seen as something that happens early in life and in disciplinary chunks but as an ongoing continuous process, in which the learner retains responsibility for, and control of, its progress. At the formal education stage, personal tutors can be the key people to explore this process with students. They have the expertise to help them make connections between themselves as learners and the formal education process.

This chapter explores the concept of 'knowing self' and 'knowing self as a learner' and discusses why it is important that the tutor facilitates and fosters this particular concept of self in promoting the process of learning. In it, we suggest there are two routes to gaining a better knowledge of yourself:

- personal reflection; and
- self-assessment and evaluation.

A key element of both these processes is discussion and feedback. In the first, tutors help students to reflect on themselves as learners. In the second, they help students to use that knowledge to make judgements about future actions.

We explore, within the context of other theories about self-understanding and self-assessment, what 'knowing self as a learner' might mean and how personal reflection helps development. In Chapter 4 we describe the experiences of teachers and lecturers who have supported their students beyond the confines of a subject area towards an understanding of themselves as learners in a generic sense. In doing so we consider the implications for the teaching-learning interface within whole groups, small groups and one-to-one situations, and for enabling the individual to map their preferred routes towards specific learning goals.

What do we mean by 'knowing yourself'?

Knowing yourself does not seem like an onerous or insurmountable task. Some might question whether it rates a chapter in a book about learning. As individuals, and in western cultures in general, we tend to think that having a good personal understanding is fairly easy and uncomplicated. If we consider it at all, we think it is something passive that just happens to us. Most of us would claim that we hold a true and realistic picture of ourselves that, if anything, is somewhat modest. As we grow older we often acknowledge that how we see ourselves does not always match the way we present ourselves to the world. But how true a picture (or pictures) our own view is, or how we use that knowledge to advance our understanding of how we learn, is not something that we often put to the test. Although a certain degree of self-knowledge can develop, inevitably, as a result of life events and experiences, some of us require nurturing and guidance in attaining effective levels of objective self-awareness and analysis. Just as factual and theoretical understanding require confirmation, reasoning and explication through interactions with other people, good personal understanding is not merely derived from innate knowledge and skills, but is aided by informed reflection, practice and guidance. These are complex skills that can require deconstruction and nurturing.

We are what we think we are

We know that how we see ourselves can affect our performance. Bandura's self-efficiency theory (Bandura 1986 in Shen and Pedulla 2000) suggests that a high self-perception of capability leads to high levels of motivation (effort and persistence) and ultimately to high levels of achievement. The process is cyclical in that high levels of achievement lead to even greater self-perception of one's capabilities which leads to greater goals being set, the willingness to expend more effort, greater persistence and perseverance, more resilience to failure and so on. However, Shen and Pedulla, from their cross-national study using data from the Third International Mathematics and Science Study (TIMSS), challenge the relationship between perceptions of capability and performance – high-achieving Japanese students scored low on perceptions of their capability to do well in the tests with the reverse being true for students in some western countries. Others (e.g. Fouzder and Markwick 2000) would suggest that students who see success as being within their control (e.g. Asian students' belief that greater effort on their part will lead to greater achievement) are more likely to adopt appropriate learning strategies. Bornholt (2000) suggests that self-stereotyping in adolescents can affect their academic achievement and career choice. He describes how important it is for the adolescent to develop both a sense of individuality and one of belonging. It is the tension between these that can lead to self-stereotyping: wanting to be different but also part of the group. Students will compare themselves against the 'prototypical' group member and develop perceptions of themselves that can affect their performance at school and beyond. For example, the perception by some adolescents of girls' and boys' subjects can lead to choices that have nothing to do with ability. Bornholt's work extends that of Byrne and Shavelson (1986) on the academic self-concept in relation to specific subject areas. They suggest that the academic self-concept, a subset of the more general self-concept, also has its own subsets in relation to subject areas such as English, mathematics and science. Their work shows that academic self-concept in relation to different subject areas is distinguishable from level of performance in that subject but correlated with it. They also suggest that, while at an early age the subject area self-concepts are interrelated, they become more independent as the student gets older. How a student sees him or herself in relation to a specific subject area – perceptions of their competence in mathematics, and their sense of belonging to a community of mathematicians (Wood 1998) for example – can affect whether or not they see themselves as maths learners. If students are to avoid this self-stereotyping, the role of the teacher becomes one of facilitating the development of positive academic self-concepts in relation to their particular subject area.

Developments in this sense of self can be described as 'understanding one's idiosyncratic personal characteristics with the requirements of inter-personal relations' (Damon 1983 in Bornholt 2000: 416). In this we would include the ability to:

- observe yourself and recognize your values, strengths and weaknesses;
- articulate and explain your feelings and aspirations;
- articulate and plan your actions and reactions; and
- understand the relationships between thoughts, values, feelings and actions.

Good communication and feedback are crucial in helping others achieve personal understanding, in identifying their own strengths and weaknesses and in achieving desired goals. But we would argue that these aspects are generic skills and need to be developed as such. There is a danger in relating key skills too closely to specific subject areas. The relationship between the teacher and the student can create a situation where a positive academic self-concept is only associated with particular subjects and not with a perception of the self as a learner. This, in itself, can lead to self-stereotyping and rejection of some aspects of learning. We would never assume that there is one 'right' practice for learning. Each task generates a different way of learning for every individual and individuals will use different learning techniques for different tasks at different life stages. A personal understanding that enables students to consider and select an appropriate strategy for a particular learning situation, and also allows them to make informed judgements about the effectiveness of their learning, as opposed to achievement in a particular subject, is crucial. We would therefore argue that enabling students to develop a sense of identity as learners, rather than as learners of mathematics, English and so on, plus an understanding of what that means, is an important part of promoting lifelong learning. We discuss below how the skills to develop a concept of self as a learner can be fostered through discussion with, and feedback from, others.

Talking about yourself

The key element in knowing yourself is personal reflection. We would argue that this is a skill that can be learned and improved. We think that the reality for many students is that, until a discussion with their tutor is looming, they will not have reflected on their sense of identity as a learner, or if they have, they will not have articulated it in such a way as to be useful. We therefore begin by exploring how and why discussion with a tutor can be the starting point for reflection and lead to self-understanding.

In 1986, Harris and Bell observed that good communication about work motivates learners, while in their study into the benefits of student talk, Rudduck *et al.* (1996) stated that relationships at school are an important influence affecting students' attitudes to their learning. MacBeath *et al.* (1996), in their seminal work on school self-evaluation, highlighted students' need for support and good quality relationships with informed adults. Rudduck *et al.* noted that it was apparent that students valued the teacher-student relationship particularly when teachers were available to talk to students about their learning and schoolwork. Claxton (1990: 107) further supported these ideas in identifying talk as an important strategy for learning: 'If you can talk to your teachers, or your Mum and Dad or, most importantly, your friends about school work you may be in a more powerful position than those who cannot'.

However, to be effective, one-to-one discussions must be focused on individual learning. Teachers are not counsellors. Nor should they be. There are school and college procedures, supporting agencies and legal parameters for issues beyond the personal and professional scope of the teacher. While there may be a case for specialists in the counselling area, classroom practitioners should be primarily concerned with learning. Good one-to-one discussions aim to help students explore their current successes and disappointments; make explicit their feelings and attitudes about where they are now; and then plan future action. Strategies for achieving this will not be the same for each student and some students will benefit more than others. At its most effective, such a discussion can promote self-awareness and self-confidence, opportunity awareness and the development of planning skills at all stages of learning. At its minimal level, the dialogue can become an interview that helps individuals select appropriate options at a particular phase in their lives. At its worst, it can be an intrusion into private matters. Unless both participants see it as closely focused on the student as learner its purpose becomes vague and confused.

From an early age, children respond and react to feedback from their parents, teachers and peers. Adult response can, however, be authoritarian, negative and unsystematic; whereas feedback from peers is often unrealistic and emotional. The information gleaned from unstructured conversation can be unconsciously self-selected and, hence, what is assimilated may be only one version of the reality. Structure, reinforcement and capability are needed to build up a true picture. Capability is required from both participants in a dialogue: the person giving the feedback and also from the one receiving it. In the quest for self-understanding, feedback needs to be both accurate and acceptable. The student must be able to assimilate the new knowledge into their current self-portrait and, if necessary, adjust the picture. In a study concerned with the mentoring of student primary teachers, Hayes (2001) found that the students who prospered were those who had feedback from their host teachers that was specific, acknowledging strengths and weaknesses but in such as way as to suggest strategies for addressing problems. Feedback, and its accompanying discussion, needs to be used to engage the learner in the process of making explicit the connections between their own instinctive, intuitive ways of learning and the more formal, outcome-focused learning of the classroom. Feedback also helps personal reflection that, in turn, enables students to make better judgements about the effectiveness of their learning strategies.

In our research we found very little evidence that tutors discussed *how* to explore strategies for better learning with their students. Although the relationship between tutor and student is clearly a factor in effective learning, in the main, both parties failed to maximize the wider benefits for learning about their own styles and preferences and for using these in the learning context. A one-to-one student-centred dialogue is not, by itself, a blueprint for learning about yourself as a learner and often the connections need to be made explicit.

Tutors, often more than students themselves, welcomed the dialogues for the level of insight they provided about their students' perceptions, experiences and difficulties. However, the important role the tutors have here is in reflecting that insight back to students in such a way as to enable them to develop a better understanding of themselves as learners. In the most propitious cases, such insights allowed teachers to be more confident in providing the appropriate scaffolding to help the student plan their learning. However, there is a vital step in connecting that scaffolding to the student's own perceptions and experiences. Unless this is made explicit the tutor is in danger of retaining control of the learning process. For example, in a study using metaphor to explore students' concepts of their learning in chemistry (Thomas and McRobbie 1999) one student described her learning as a maze with a range of opportunities, some of which would prove to be dead ends. However, this same student did not see it as her responsibility to find her way through the maze but the role of the teacher to show her the way. Understanding which false starts the student is likely to take may be helpful to the teacher in planning his or her teaching strategies but unless that is shared with the student and the student also understands and can see the bigger picture she or he is unlikely to gain a clearer sense of self and their own 'idiosyncratic personal characteristics' (Damon 1983 in Bornholt 2000) as a learner. This reflecting back to students how their own perceptions help the teacher to suggest ways forward would appear to be an important part of the feedback.

Controlling the discussion

As we said in Chapter 2, it is important that the dialogue should be, at least partly, within the control of the student. Most classroom discourse is at the invitation of the teacher (see Norman 1992) and conducted in an open forum. Activities such as one-to-one tutorials for planning learning put students in a different relationship with their tutors, and remove the distraction or influence of the peer group. It should not be assumed, however, that the perceptions of tutors and students are the same. Although most tutors in our research saw one-to-one discussions as a student-led process, a number of students saw them as a school or college process (often before making option choices) with the tutors asking questions and setting the agenda. The students commented that 'the tutor asks questions' while a few tutors observed that students found it hard to talk to them. Unless the student is fully engaged in the process in the sense of retaining some power and control, it will always remain a 'teaching' situation rather than one of 'learning' (Fielding 2001).

It was apparent that there were some tutors who found this difficult. Making the connections between a process that was focused on involving students in their learning and the increasing expectation in schools and colleges for improved performance, was a real point of tension for the teachers. In our research (Bullock and Wikeley 1999), this tension was often expressed in terms of the uneasy relationship between personal learning targets (an outcome of this particular process) and more subject-oriented targets. Teachers see themselves as just that – 'teachers' – and handing over some of the power to students in order to let them create an understanding of themselves as learners (which will not always match that of the teacher) can be antithetical to their established values and practice, and hence a courageous step.

Self-assessment and evaluation

Some (see Boud 1995) believe that self-assessment is the key to effective lifelong learning. The skill of successful self-assessment is an important progression from personal understanding. Learning is a developmental process and knowing when your understanding has moved on, and when it has not, is a vital characteristic of learning. Personal understanding allows individuals to ascertain their own effectiveness in any action and to inform choices that will build on strengths and address weaknesses. For young people, there is now an abundance of educational and personal opportunities. All too often, immaturity and lack of realistic self-assessment results in ill-informed decision making with inappropriate paths selected (see Palmer 2001) and learning diminished.

Gathering evidence

Approaching this in an objective manner (although it is obviously essentially a subjective judgement) involves gathering evidence in order to make judgements about the quality of your own efforts and the potentiality of making improvements; that is, it has a formative dimension. The role of the tutor, usually in a one-to-one discussion, is to provide a non-judgemental opportunity for students to identify, discuss objectively and value the evidence for assessing their own progress, either in subject areas or in generic learning skills.

Self-understanding is therefore an important factor in being able to evaluate critically your own efforts. However, students are more used to having their activities appraised and assessed by their teachers. They see this as a means of identifying what they have attained (or learned) and use it as a normative comparison of their own outcomes and behaviours in relation to that of their peers. Positive outcomes from this may be superficial and short-lived while disappointing results can be seriously demotivating and discouraging. The increased use of performance data within schools and colleges and their publication, both locally and nationally, creates a benchmark system whereby students judge their own success primarily in terms of outcomes and in comparison with others. However, knowing whether or not your externally assessed performance exceeds that of your peers does not particularly help in the processes of learning. It is the ability to judge your current performance against the reality of your potential performance that is crucial.

In general, students are not prepared for assessing and judging their own actions with a view to identifying areas of strength and weakness that can be used to improve their own learning. For learning to be effective, learners need to be able to recognize the constituents of their own 'best effort' and to identify their own route to attaining that. They need to compare strategies and discuss standards with others so that they can rationalize and articulate their self-evaluations. Self-assessment, therefore, cannot take place in isolation. Like learning, it needs to occur in relationship with others (Boud 1995).

Many students' understanding of the concepts of critical thinking and evaluation is both limited and unsophisticated, focusing on criticism (often negative) and being sceptical (Bailin *et al.* 1999). This may not be surprising. Even postgraduate students in higher education can be unsure of the processes involved in critical discourse (Wallace and Poulson 2003) and need clear guidance in becoming self-critical. At the secondary school level, students find difficulty in shifting from the perception that questioning and evaluation is something done *to* them rather than something that should be done *by* them. How much harder this is when applying it to your own way of learning.

Understanding the criteria

In order to assess your own efforts it is necessary, first, to understand the appropriate criteria which should be applied in each case. Unless you know what counts as good work, it is impossible to judge your own. Despite teachers' concern that a good piece of written work should, for example, demonstrate a coherent argument, research shows that uncritical students invariably believe content and presentation to be most important to the assessment criteria (Bullock *et al.* 2002). Students tend to equate more effort with more writing and hence the achievement of higher grades: their view is that 'more equals better'. In one of our research projects (Bullock *et al.* 2002), when asked how they might improve their coursework, students responded that better coursework would have been more detailed, would have had more time spent on it and would be better presented in terms of spelling and grammar.

In many programmes (e.g. GCSE coursework and other assessed project work) students are required, explicitly, to evaluate their own work. Although some students acknowledge that critical and creative learning (indicated by structure, argument and understanding) will 'get them marks', few know how to show it by demonstrating that they have answered the question and evaluated their own efforts. Teachers agree that the evaluation requirement of assessed project work demands engagement with critical thinking processes, and they acknowledge the difficulties in preparing their students effectively for this. Not all teachers feel that the development of critical evaluation skills is a readily attainable goal for particular students at the secondary school stage (Martin *et al.* 2002) and it is clear that more emphasis and explication of the activities and the steps that are appropriate in assessing and evaluating your own performance are required:

> They [students] can be led to achieve reasonable standards in describing their data, but when it comes to analysing it and giving evaluations of it, then it becomes far more difficult … It's the evaluation where they need most help and where they're looking at a particular hypothesis – where they've collected their results and they come to explain it, we say to them, 'Have you found evidence to support or reject that hypothesis? Has your information confirmed what you expected? Is it true or false?' and I like to think it's a court case, I like to put them in the position of being in court and saying, 'Have you proved or disproved this particular theory?' and think of it in those terms. I think they do appreciate that and understand it, although again you may get a shorter answer rather than a longer one. But at least we get them to actually question whether they've gathered enough evidence or not.
>
> (Geography teacher, comprehensive school)

Some schools provide their students with highly structured templates of how an evaluation should be written. Others feel that enabling strategies, such as discussions and explanations of the nature and processes of critical evaluation, allow students to develop critical skills more fully. The key aim is encouraging personal engagement and honest self-appraisal. It should help the student recognize the difference between their capabilities for learning and the label given by their latest mark sheet. Subject teachers tend to predict future performance by past performance, but students need a realistic understanding of themselves in which judgements are based on knowledge about whether, for example, a piece of work has been a struggle or was dashed off in five minutes in front of the television. The tutor's role is to help students face these realities and to come to a better understanding of their true potential.

The context for enabling self-evaluation can be crucial, and here the personal tutor has a major role in helping students take an overview of all their attainments. We found that students, working in subject areas at the whole-class or at the individual level, often associate critical thinking with high stress situations. Teacher-student interactions that monitor the quality of work are frequently seen to be situations where the 'cards are stacked' in the teacher's favour and can be perceived by students as confrontations and apparent challenges to their individuality and identity. Although subject teachers work to encourage self-critical and evaluative skills such as questioning prior knowledge and experience, testing out and applying new knowledge, and promoting learner responsibility through reflection and evaluation, even capable students fail to associate these skills with successful learning across the curriculum. Most regard the skills as particular to the specific subject, or even activity.

In contrast, student-student interactions in small-group work (e.g. discussing texts and media in English or carrying out fieldwork in geography) are valued by students as unthreatening and more conducive to fostering the skills of critical thinking and self-understanding (Morehouse 1997). Students feel that, in small groups, they can share their work without reservation. Informal comparison with the efforts of their classmates allows them to identify the critical indicators of quality. If tutors are to be successful in nurturing skills of self-assessment and evaluation they need to recreate the safe, equitable environment of the student-student groups while using their own experience to create more challenge. The non-threatening approach of many local education authorities or districts to the introduction of teacher appraisal comes to mind (Wragg *et al.* 1996).

Conclusions

In this chapter we have explored the key elements in helping students come to a better understanding of themselves as learners. These are the skills of personal reflection, self-assessment and evaluation. We argue that these techniques need to be learned and practised. They are a vital part of becoming a successful adult learner and should not be left to chance. Students in the 14 to 19 age range are coming to terms with the social complexities of the adult world, and at the same time they are having to cope with a formal education system that will be a major influence on their future lives. As Gray (1995) stressed, one of the three indicators of an effective school is that each student has a vital relationship with, at least, one teacher. The personal tutor can be that teacher if the 'vital' relationship focuses on true dialogue, but helps both student and tutor grow in their understanding of self. Developing these skills of personal reflection and self-assessment cannot be understated.

4 Helping students to know themselves

Researcher: *Obviously it's personal, but what sort of targets are they?*

Female 4: *Mine was to talk less and listen more, which I haven't achieved yet.*

Female 2: *Mine was maths because the teachers teach at other people's standards and not to mine. So I just had a private word with her and said, 'If I don't understand, when I get stuck can I ask you?' So I did that instead of just sitting there shyly and not doing anything. Ever since then I've worked on that.*

Researcher: *What was the target you wrote down?*

Female 1: *I just put, 'Don't be too confused when I've got a problem. Ask.'*
(Year 9 students, comprehensive school)

Introduction

In this chapter we offer practical examples of how schools and colleges can organize opportunities for students to formulate and express knowledge of themselves and to use this emerging self-knowledge as a springboard for their learning. Although one of the key findings from our own research (Bullock and Wikeley 1999) was that the success of the PLP project lay in the fact that it was universal and did not target one particular group of students (e.g. the underachievers or disaffected boys), we also found that it was exactly these groups that benefited most and who claimed they were most likely to use the strategies for planning their learning in the future. Our findings indicate that other groups of students are more likely to already use a wide variety of peers and other adults to support their learning. They are experienced in the ways of discussing themselves with others and using conversations with a range of people not only to gather information but also to test out ideas about themselves and plan for their futures. In Bourdieu's terms (Bourdieu and Passeron 1990) these groups of students have the cultural capital to take full advantage of formal education. Others, however, do not. For these students the idea that they have control of their learning is new. They see themselves very much as 'the taught' rather than as 'learners'. For this group the personal tutor is vital to support them in making connections between the formal education process and life as they experience it (now and in the future).

To show how this educational relationship can work we have gathered examples of noteworthy one-to-one and small group tutorial activities from tutors in a wide range of schools and colleges. The activities described have been used by tutors to help students to know themselves as learners. In some cases the activities could equally, and may even be, cited in Chapters 6 and 8 as being about content or strategies for learning, but we make no apology for that, for as will be seen in Chapter 9 we argue that the three aspects of learning are tightly interlinked. However, in this chapter the emphasis is on how the strategies can be used to help students know themselves, to see learning as a process that needs to be personalized if it is to be successful. The tutors, whose practice is described here, saw their role as being to help students articulate their strengths and weaknesses, and to explain their likes and dislikes in ways that would allow them to see the links with their ideas and plans for future learning. It is an educational relationship in which the tutor uses his or her greater knowledge and experience to challenge and support the student's own reflections about him or herself and in so doing helps the student to move forward.

Our observations suggest that these educational relationships deserve thorough preparation and critical review. The most effective experiences involve planning, interaction and revisiting by both students and tutors. We give examples of how personal reflection can be presented as a tool for learning and offer strategies that tutors might use to encourage students' critical thinking to self-evaluate and make realistic judgements about their achievements. We highlight the need for tutors to participate overtly in the process of learning by modelling themselves as learners. Again we are not advocating that tutors are the only people who engage with students in this way. Our research shows very clearly the use students make of parents, friends, siblings and even siblings' boyfriends and girlfriends as knowledgeable others who can advise and guide them in their learning journeys, but where this is not happening the tutor has an even more crucial part to play.

The theoretical arguments for our suggestions are set out in the previous chapter. As we suggest in that discussion, there is no right way to begin when helping students to know themselves as learners. The best starting point will depend on the individual student and ultimately on that student retaining some sense of being at least an equal contributor to the discussion with the personal tutor. In the busy world of schools and colleges, tutors will have to make the most of the opportunities that are available within the constraints of timetables and their current knowledge of their students. Our framework presents ideas for consideration rather than a recipe for success. We offer it as a contribution to reflective practice that, in turn, creates a model for reflective learning.

The compulsion for outcomes

One of the difficulties for teachers in helping their students know themselves as learners is that the teachers are focused on outcomes and are seen by students to be so. This was one of the main issues for schools involved in the PLP project (Bullock and Wikeley 1999). While personal learning was intended as a process-driven activity the tutors often gave the students the impression that it was the 'prizes' for learning that counted. As one interviewee put it when told by her tutor that she needed to 'correct' the written version of her Personal Learning Plan because she had not included, when listing her strengths, the prizes she had won for her dancing:

Female: That's not learning … it's just something I do.

Researcher: What would you count as learning?

Female: Like when your parents get divorced and you have to learn how to live with your dad separately from your mum.
                                (Year 11 student, comprehensive school)

Although it is obvious that the tutor's intentions were well meant, the student clearly had a different understanding from the tutor about learning as a process. When presented with a student who was not an academic high flyer, the tutor wanted to make sure that she recorded everything that showed her to her best advantage and acknowledged her out of school achievements as being as valid as academic ones. For the student, personal learning was about being able to cope with life as it is, changing ways of behaving that acknowledged life's realities, not prizes she collected for her leisure activities. In helping the student understand that both aspects of learning have their place, it would have been helpful for this tutor to explore the student's understanding of her learning and personal development from this experience, rather than merely instruct her to rewrite her plan. It is the skill of personalizing learning within the context of your whole life that we think is so important.

One vital element in making this happen is the tutors' own engagement with the process. In some schools where the purposes and objectives of the one-to-one tutorials were discussed and clarified among contributing staff teams, they became fully aware of their own perceptions of learning and themselves as learners. In order to help their students understand themselves as learners it appeared that the tutors had to model the experience themselves.

Types of tutors

From our work with teachers in the PLP project we identified three levels of tutor engagement with the process. This applied both to working with students and also when working with us (researchers) in evaluating the initiative. While there are positive achievements and merit at each of these levels of interaction with students, we suggest that it is worth considering where tutors sit on this continuum as this may be helpful in moving tutorial discussions and activities to be more centred on learning.

Jumping through hoops

The first level we call 'jumping through hoops' because these tutors appear not to move beyond engaging with the structure of the process itself. They see the action plan as a product that needs to be elicited from the students, and they appear not to envisage wider benefits beyond a prescribed outcome-oriented approach. The tutors operating at this level often see the setting of targets as the object of the exercise rather than as a context within which to develop more usable learning skills and strategies. Although they view learning as an active process as far as students' efforts will support better outcomes, they have a detached view of school learning. These tutors might suggest the following as evidence of effective learning:

- improved examination/test results, preferably using some notion of value-added;
- appropriate future destinations;
- better quality careers office/guidance interviews;
- better quality curriculum vitae being produced;
- students initiating the use of careers resources and the frequency of usage.

All these represent an outcome, external objectives view of learning. Although such an approach is obviously part of a larger picture, and all tutors operate to some extent with this agenda, for some this appears to be their only endeavour. It matches the view of students who see the whole initiative as yet another school process with which to comply. Such students talk of the increasing expectation in schools for improved performance and how that takes precedence over the more personal nature of their learning. It does not connect with the idea that students need to know themselves as learners in order to own their own learning. Rather than seeing learning as a social, collaborative act it could be construed that tutors see learning as a competition with the most worthy students winning the prizes. An example of this occurred in one PLP school where the process appeared centred on the completion of the action plan or document. The meeting between the pupil and tutor did not occur until the plan was written in draft and the one-to-one dialogue focused on the document, the personal statement and the targets set by the pupil. Pupils regarded this dialogue as a marking process that emphasized for them the school-directed nature of PLP.

Getting to know you

The second level of engagement embraces those teachers who are positive about the concept of personal tutoring (the majority) but who see the process, mainly, as a way of getting to know their students better. From our PLP interviews, it was clear that tutors greatly value the one-to-one interviews in Year 9 (see also Rudduck *et al.* 1996). The school coordinators (staff who were appointed to lead the initiative in each school) reported that tutors felt that the dialogue helped them to get to know students quicker and better, and this had nurtured positive relationships between staff and students. Particular benefits are that the one-to-one interview distinguishes the relatively quiet group of average attainers, provides quicker support strategies for those who are struggling, and makes identification of specific needs easier: 'You don't know them very well until one-to-one' (Year 9 tutor, comprehensive school).

Those directly involved with PLP felt that, after the one-to-one interview, more Year 9 students had given thought to their future, where they wanted to be and what they needed to do to get there. For some students, conducting an individual conversation with an adult outside the family is a real step forward in communication skills. There is also some evidence from our data that boys, more than girls, gain more directly from the one-to-one discussion with their tutor and that the personal dialogue raises boys' skills and confidence in thinking and talking about their own strengths and weaknesses. PLP school coordinators suggested that this was partly a function of the earlier maturing and skills of reflection in adolescent girls. At age 13, boys entered PLP with greater reluctance to analyse and plan their lives and the impact of the one-to-one conversation with a tutor might, therefore, have been more significant: 'At first they won't even look an adult in the eye and are struggling to get words out, but at the end of it they're actually making eye contact, talking more confidently' (Year 9 tutor, comprehensive school).

Higher ability students appear to benefit less from the one-to-one tutorials but often talk of other adults with whom they discuss their plans for the future and their learning. This is not to say that they do not enjoy talking with their tutors; they just fail to make the connection between the tutorials and their much broader view of the learning process.

'Getting to know you' tutors acknowledge the complexity and transferability of learning and might suggest the following as evidence of effective learning:

- the ability of students to make informed choices about Year 11 courses, work experience options and careers;
- the identification of and setting of SMART targets (see Chapter 6).

However, learning about students is not the same as learning about their learning skills and habits. In our research, there was very little reporting of how tutors had explored strategies for learning with the students. It would appear that hearing about students' lives outside school is regarded by some teachers as the factor that will enable them to improve their students' achievement. It is not completely clear whether it is the knowing that is important or the students sharing that knowledge that makes it important. This is equally unclear for some students, and occasionally resentment is expressed that the questioning in tutorials is too personal.

However interesting and useful 'getting to know you' may be for the tutors, it is not particularly helpful for the student, or at least it does not help them know themselves as learners. Although many of the students we have talked to enjoy the tutor showing interest in their lives, others can find it quite intrusive, and very few see any connection between it and improving their learning. There are two reasons for this. First, exchange of information is never two-way. The tutor is interested in the student's life but does not expect to answer questions about his or her own life. This gives very clear messages about who has control of the agenda. Second, the student will present their life in a way that they think is acceptable to the tutor, but in doing so will not be reflecting on how those experiences relate to the way they learn now or could learn in the future. At best, such conversations help the tutor explain why the student is, or is not, achieving and at worst they encourage defensiveness.

The reflective tutor

Where the personal tutorial is most effective the tutors are operating at a third level of engagement. This third level, which we call that of the 'reflective tutor', involves the tutors engaging with the process as an experience of their own personal learning. The crucial factor is the tutor's conceptualization of the nature of learning and of him or herself as a learner. Effective tutors appreciate that they, themselves, have become better learners as a result of the tutoring experience (see also Philip and Hendry 2000). Their efforts to make the learning process meaningful to students requires them to reflect on their own learning processes. This activity increases the tutor's awareness of models and patterns of learning and consequently helps them to develop the ability to see problems in new and different ways.

These tutors are more likely to have a personal, developmental view of learning and would cite the following as evidence of effective learning:

- raised self-esteem and self-confidence;
- improved ability in meeting and communicating short-term goals;
- improved ability in assessing and articulating strengths and weaknesses and setting realistic goals in all areas (personal/social academic/vocational);
- improved interpersonal skills – individual and group, with peers, tutor, parents or carers and subject staff;
- more positive reporting and fewer sanctions.

Such tutors do not reject the more outcome-oriented view of learning but see it as only a part of the whole process, and perhaps a less important part when trying to help students to take responsibility for their own learning.

Establishing a genuine dialogue

Talking to students about their learning in a personal way is not something that many teachers feel prepared for. The tutorial may cover strategies for learning and the relevance of course content for future ambitions, but it needs to be focused at the personal level and the centrality of the one-to-one dialogue in learning about self needs to be continuously stressed. How tutors establish a genuine dialogue with individual students, and the strategies they use to offer helpful but challenging feedback, are varied. Once again we stress that there is no 'right' way but offer ideas for consideration and development.

For the tutorial to be an effective learning opportunity, the dialogue between a student and a tutor needs to have a clear purpose and structure. Our discussions and interviews with tutors and senior managers have identified a weak spot between most tutors' assertion that the dialogue with students is enlightening and enjoyable, and the claim from learning co-ordinators or pastoral managers that many are not able to make the most of the discussion in terms of helping their students to understand themselves as learners. This also matches students' perceptions that tutorials are a school activity and tutor-led: 'The tutor asks the questions and I answer' (Year 9 female student, comprehensive school).

Some tutors do, however, use strategies explicitly designed to engage the student in conversation about themselves as a learner. They invite their students to explain their daily routines and achievements; the organization of their learning; and their motivations for learning. They encourage students to think of themselves as unique; to consider how they learn best; and to identify any particular problems related to their learning. They encourage students to think broadly and to articulate how they feel about learning. This, of course, presupposes that there is a common understanding of what learning is, but the best tutors understand that learning is a complex and ongoing task and often offer their own experiences of being a learner as part of the reflection process. This model of learning from a more capable other can be particularly empowering. Tutors discuss specific skills and requirements with students – for example, what they need to know in order to meet the criteria for tests and examinations such as the General National Vocational Qualification (GNVQ) or GCSE – but always personalize the conversation by referring to the particular student's way of learning.

Priorities in these discussions are identified here.

- Helping develop a common understanding about individual learning styles and strategies. Asking how, why, and what if?
  - Describe an experience that you think of as learning.
  - Was it successful and what made it so?
  - Could you have done anything differently and felt even more successful?
- Encouraging students to clarify what they feel about themselves as individuals and learners (not to probe into innermost thoughts but to emphasize that learning is emotional as well as practical).
  - How do you feel about your work in X class? Who do you work with? Who do you ask for help?
  - How do you feel when you have homework to do for Y? How do you feel when you have completed it?
- Extending students' ideas, thoughts and feelings about learning by offering metaphors, different words and phrases, or by reflecting back the students' talk to them.
  - Do you mean that … ?
  - Have I understood you correctly … ?
  - That sounds as though you are describing a journey. Is that how you see it?

Although tutors will always talk about the importance of the dialogue being controlled or led by the student, this is never easy to manage. Research shows that many students feel that the one-to-one tutorial initiative is a school procedure set up to facilitate better organization and control and is there for the benefit of the school: 'There wasn't any talking in it. We just had to say what we'd like to achieve and what we'd like to stop doing' (Year 9 male student, comprehensive school).

Where students are well prepared for the one-to-one session and have discussed its aims and purposes, and where there has been reflection on and sharing of tutor skills, discussions begin to move towards student control or at least towards the idea that they are equal contributors. The skills tutors need to promote a shared power base, include those of negotiation. It is important to negotiate with the student, within clearly explained parameters, the format of the tutorial by agreeing its purposes and outcomes, and the when and the where.

The role of the tutor is to help the student understand that the tutorial is not purely a school-generated activity. However, there needs to be an honesty in the dialogue, that acknowledges the relationship between tutor and tutee: the ultimate power will always rest with the tutor. As it is taking place within the context of school or college the tutorial will always have a focus on improving formal learning. But working within this context, the aim is to help the student make sense of their whole experience as a learner and to help them judge how effective they have been in the learning task.

We have always been struck when talking to young people about their learning by their high motivation to succeed. This often appears to be at odds with teacher and media views that young people today lack motivation. We would argue that it is helping students access that intrinsic motivation and desire to achieve by relating to all aspects of their learning, in and out of school, that is a sign of an effective tutor. Getting students to talk about their learning, challenging their views in a constructive way and helping them make connections between their lives in and out of school, is the essence of a genuine dialogue.

As we argued in the previous chapter, a major aspect of one-to-one discussions is feedback. This enables students to evaluate their efforts realistically. Experienced tutors believe that giving feedback is the most crucial factor in helping students to understand themselves as learners. It is not always easy to accomplish effectively. For feedback to be worthwhile, it needs to be specific, honest, positive and challenging. For example, 'I would agree that … but your last test shows that …'

Feedback needs to be offered to the student as part of a two-way conversation and be accepted as sensible, fair and appropriate. Tutors need to ensure that they listen carefully to the student's perspective before and while feedback is being offered. Unless the student can recognize him or herself in whatever the tutor is offering they will become defensive and disengage from the conversation.

From our experience we suggest that feedback from a tutor is different from feedback from parents or peers. The unique position of a tutor allows an overview of educational systems, learning and assessment to which others are not necessarily privy. Tutors have an understanding of the whole cohort of young people and a knowledge of the individual interactions and relationships within the 'classroom' group. This can be both an advantage and a disadvantage. While students have, or should have, a holistic view of their learning and how they experience learning both in and out of the school or college setting, the tutors only see them in that formal setting. However, it is in the formal setting that progress needs to be made and made effectively. It is this that is at the core of the tutor-tutee educational relationship. The tutor, with greater knowledge of how to progress in the system, can support the student to make connections between and benefit from various experiences of learning. The purpose of feedback is to provide the structures for improvement and development. It therefore needs to be timely. We have observed tutors using a range of tutorial and teaching activities to provide the appropriate regular, ongoing feedback. Guidelines, derived from conversations and interviews with a range of tutors for giving effective feedback in a one-to-one tutorial might include the following elements.

Feedback needs to be specific. Too often, in our experience, students receive feedback that urges them to *work harder, pay more attention, spend more time on task*. This is not necessarily helpful for students who frequently have a hazy conception of the reality of these exhortations. (When asked how they might have obtained better grades, students, too, expressed ways of improving in these generalized terms.) Students need to know exactly what they can do in order to learn more effectively (the strategies), but they need to personalize it. For example, *working harder* for one student might mean spending more time reading around the subject but for another it might mean discussing what has been covered in class with another student in order to make sense of what has been offered. For a third it could translate into handing homework in by the deadline. *Spending more time on task* could mean sorting out ideas in your head before sharing with someone else or using the discussion with another person to get the ideas straight. Students who know that they find it difficult to take in complicated instructions might need to think about negotiating strategies with their teachers for checking at a later stage whether they have understood correctly:

Researcher: What was the target you wrote down?

Female: I just put 'don't be confused when I've got a problem. Ask'.
(Year 9 student, comprehensive school)

Another commonly given piece of tutor feedback is *to read more widely*. In specific terms, this means that students need to think about how to organize and focus their time for reading; to give themselves time to reflect; and reconstruct and make links with knowledge from other sources. In particular, students need to know what is meant by 'critical and analytical reading'. Such analyses of texts are often modelled by teachers as they present arguments for the meaning and logic of readings, but the underlying steps in scrutinizing, thinking and drawing conclusions may not always be explicitly set out for students. The personal tutorial is an opportunity to explore which aspects of reading for learning the student finds difficult or even which aspects they avoid or just don't do. The tutor, as the more competent 'other' (Vygotsky in Daniels 1996), can help students explore what it is about themselves that makes this difficult.

We are not suggesting that a tutor would offer all these strategies, but in helping a student know which are the most appropriate for him or herself they form a basis for discussion enabling the student to articulate a personal interpretation of such generalized advice. In this context, understanding yourself is as important as understanding the peculiarities of the subject area.

Feedback needs to be positive. In our research, tutors were very aware that all feedback (good and not so good) should be given sensitively. As far as possible, negative comments were tempered with suggestions for improvement and these were often sought from students in the belief that this would encourage them to feel more in control of the discussion. Such tutors made a point of listening to and respecting the students' rationale and points of view. Students were also invited to analyse and ask questions about the tutor's judgements and perspectives.

When helping students to know themselves it is important to remember that only a few people overestimate their own capabilities. Students are much more likely to express a negative estimation of their potential achievement than an over-positive one:

Tutor 1:   I find particularly I'm emphasizing them telling me what their achievements are, because so many of them just don't want to talk about it. They don't even write it down, even though there's a box that says 'Achievements'.

Tutor 2:   They don't recognize their achievements.

Tutor 1:   They don't want to put their qualities down.

Tutor 2:   They're not used to writing a personal statement. As I say, it's the process that's important because when they come to UCAS [Universities Council for Admission of Students] or for an employer, by the time we've done PLP and NRA

[National Records of Achievement], etc., they are used to writing about themselves. PLP is the toe in the water if you like that leads on to that.

(Tutors, comprehensive school)

The one-to-one discussion is an opportunity for giving positive feedback. Even if, as occasionally happens, it is difficult to find something good to say, it is helpful to start and finish with an optimistic comment. Feedback should not be reduced to negative comparative judgements of performance because levels of confidence, motivation and enthusiasm will not be boosted by a wholly negative or disappointing one-to-one conversation. Students need to be encouraged to identify and focus on their strengths in order to build their confidence to address their real weaknesses.

Feedback needs to be challenging. In our surveys (Bullock and Wikeley 2000), many of the higher ability students saw little benefit for their learning in one-to-one discussions with their tutor. These students already know that what they are doing results in success. They have had positive feedback as a result of receiving better grades than their classmates. They already know themselves as learners, they know what works and what does not work for them and how to access help on their own terms. As others have shown (Claxton 1990; Dweck 2000) it is important, even for successful students, to have aims and goals for improvement. For such students, existing educational relationships, in and out of school, have been enough to help them know themselves. Personal tutors, therefore, can focus solely on what to learn and how to learn.

However, for other students the tutor who has built a real relationship with the student is probably the best person to give that challenging feedback. They can challenge the student's view that success is what happens to other people and emphasize that aspirations *can* be raised. Tutors are also in a position to challenge the notion that students are the victims in educational institutions, and can promote the idea that they can take control of their own learning and challenge them to do so.

Feedback needs to be honest. Part of the authority and skill of tutors is derived from their experiences of young people, educational systems, learning and assessment. They need to draw on all of this to give students feedback that is realistic and fair. Observations need to be clear and well understood. It is important to provide instances that show on what evidence the comments are based; to give the student the opportunity to offer an alternative view; and most importantly, to give that view real consideration. Although we stressed in Chapter 3 that tutors are not counsellors, counselling skills rather than interviewing skills (which are often what tutors think they need) are particularly important here. Reflecting back to the students what they have said in such a way as to make them understand the consequences of actions or the implications of their views, is an important part of helping them understand themselves.

But again we found that tutors could only act in the way described if they were also honest as to the dynamics of the relationship. Proficient tutors agreed that working with, and inducting, a novice tutor can help even the most knowledgeable teacher to reflect upon and analyse their own practice. It can remind both mentor and mentee of the nature and purpose of the personal tutorial. The educational relationship is important within a mentoring partnership, as it is within the personal tutorial. Mutual trust and respect needs to be shown but the dynamics of power need to be acknowledged. It can help set the foundations of a sound educational relationship if the tutor or mentor (with the most power) reveals something of him or herself during introductory and early sessions. For example, he or she might share their own preferred learning styles; consider their particular strengths and weaknesses as a learner; or discuss strategies they have used for problem solving. It must be remembered, however, (and this was exemplified by some tutors in the 'getting to know you' category) that the relationship between tutor and tutee or mentor and mentee is essentially an educational one. Disclosure of more personal information has to follow the lead of the least powerful (the mentee or tutee) and it is part of the role of the tutor or mentor to explain these parameters.

Preparation for the dialogue

Tutors

Careful preparation for, and induction into, the personal tutorial programme can help to raise awareness that ownership, personal development and learning are at its foundation. A preliminary task for tutors, before the most effective one-to-one and small group interviews, is to gather and reflect on evidence about the student's current achievement and progress. Tutors need to form their own picture of the student as learner, with which to clarify and challenge the student's own picture of themselves. This evidence might include:

- quantitative data such as test scores, progress reports, attendance records, previous action plans and so on; and
- qualitative data such as observations of the student (their own and other teachers'), homework, comments (verbal or written) from other teachers, communications with the student or parents and so on.

These data enable tutors to offer evidence that substantiates students' views of their own strengths and areas for development but also to challenge them when appropriate.

Some with concern for staff development have talked of the importance of tutors explicitly modelling their own learning behaviour, styles and strategies both in tutorial activities and in staff development sessions with other tutors. Learning is most frequently internal and imperceptible to others, but observable signs include the following.

- *Active listening:* giving the student or other learner undivided attention and framing the response within what has been heard.
- *Pausing:* using silences and giving the student or other learner time to think and respond.
- *Thinking out loud:* trying out unformed ideas, articulating problems, reframing thoughts, hearing and considering others' ideas and moving on.
- *Taking notes:* noting new concepts for action or future reference.

Students

One-to-one discussions flow more freely when students have thought about the nature and style of their own learning. Many tutors set a short task for students, prior to the discussion, to give them an opportunity to do this. We offer a list of examples we have come across:

- Completing a short questionnaire indicating general attitude to school or college.
- Thinking about their feelings in relation to school or college work and life in general, recording these thoughts and bringing them to the tutorial.
- Writing a self-assessment report. Students are asked to consider how well they have met recent homework tasks and deadlines, the marks they have received for assignments and outcomes of activities set out in previous action plans.
- Reflecting on themselves at school. Students note down what they like and what they do not like about their studies, plus what they feel they are good at and in what areas they would like to improve.

For reasons of time and cost some schools prepare students for one-to-one sessions with a personal tutor through focused group work. Peer tutor pairs or small groups, solely comprising students, have been used by institutions of higher and further education (Topping 1998) and also happen outside school for reflection and support. But as far as we know, this approach is rarely used in schools, where working in small groups often tends to be only a strategy for project work and prescriptive coursework tasks. In our experience, students find this form of independent learning effective and satisfying (Bullock *et al.* 2002). They benefit (as suggested above) from feedback, examples and modelling from their tutors and peers, but they still feel some sense of control. Thus it becomes a student-led process rather than an institutionally structured activity: it encourages them to see themselves as 'learners' rather than 'the taught'. When constructing these groups, most schools appear to opt for single-sex friendship groups. But it can be useful to intersperse these with selected mixes of abilities and genders. Such groups and the discussion they engender, if carefully focused, work well as a preparation for impending one-to-one tutorials. They are particularly helpful with younger groups or when it is the students' first experience of a personal discussion with their tutor. Groups can be asked to share ideas about what helps or hinders their learning, what makes them want (or not) to learn, and what makes them feel good (or not) at school.

Such group preparation can make students feel more at ease. Small groups allow everyone to be less restrained, more confident and to be heard. When meeting with their tutor one-to-one, students are able to use that confidence to engage in the conversation. Where friendship groups are used, students know each other very well and are able to support or modify perceptions of each other and add evidence from shared experiences to support or challenge the individual's view of him or herself. In small groups, students are encouraged to see each other as learners. They discuss what learning is and share their routines and strategies for learning. They compare and contrast learning experiences and develop a common vocabulary and understanding of learning. The group can provide an ongoing source of support for learning and the structured group tutorial can become an exemplar for learning conversations in other day-to-day situations.

Capturing the dialogue

Whether the outcomes of personal tutorials should be recorded or not is always a contentious issue. The main benefit of such a system is seen to be the process not the outcome. But there is an outcome and if the student is to act on the increased knowledge of themselves by changing their learning behaviour then some record that can be referred to at a later date, as part of a reflective process, is often useful:

Researcher: How do you think you'll use your written plan?

Male 2:   When I did my options I looked at it because if you haven't thought about it for a while, when you were thinking – about it – what you wrote down – so jog your memory about what you were thinking.

Male 1:   It's a good thing because when you have to write your targets, say you'd forgotten about what your targets are, you can always pick up your PLP folder, look in there and think, 'Oh yes, I tried to achieve this. Have I done it or not?' And if I haven't, what can I do to make myself achieve it?

(Year 9 students, comprehensive school)

Thought, therefore, needs to be given to providing time after the discussion for the student to reflect and make notes. Whether this record forms the basis of a review process sometime in the future is another matter for debate. We found, however, that if there is no review the benefits of the tutorial are gradually lost. In the PLP project the students wrote action plans and set targets, both personal and academic, but in many schools the most frequent complaint from students was that the targets were never reviewed or even checked for completion. It appeared that the setting of the targets became the embodiment of learning rather than the achievement of the targets themselves. When next they met their tutees, tutors often ignored what had been said previously, and the opportunity to see learning as a continuous process was lost. Not reviewing targets also gives a very clear message to students that learning is not personal nor something that needs reconsideration and reflection. Further, it fails to convey that the tutor is someone who knows them well and can help them in the reflection process. If students are to come to a real understanding of themselves as learners, it is the tutor's role to support them in making connections between past, present and future by discussing with them appropriate points for reflection.

One way forward, suggested to us, was for students to work in peer groups when writing up their learning plans after the one-to-one tutorial. This promoted the idea that learning was a social process, allowed ideas to be shared and reflected on and so promoted self-confidence. The main benefit, however, was that individual students assumed more ownership of their plans than they did with tutor-directed writing. It also seemed to offer a satisfactory cycle if students, working in peer groups to prepare for the tutorial, then returned to those peer groups to make plans for the future.

Conclusions

It is vital that before becoming involved in the personal tutorial system, tutors have had a full opportunity to explore their role, the purposes and intended outcomes of the tutorial as well as collecting enough evidence with which to challenge the students' own perceptions of themselves. We found that in one-to-one tutorials, teachers operating at 'reflective tutor' level used strategies explicitly designed to engage the student in conversations about themselves as a learner. Often this was in schools and colleges where there was a culture of staff discussing learning as a matter of course. Either formally or informally, colleagues or students were invited to explain their daily routines and achievements and their organization of and motivations for learning. Individuals were encouraged to consider how they learn best and to identify any particular problems related to their learning. Staff and students were expected to think broadly and articulate how they felt about learning.

But knowing self is not enough. In the most productive one-to-one tutorials, tutors discuss with students specific skills and what is important knowledge to meet the criteria for tests and examinations. We turn now, therefore, to the former and the support students need to develop their learning strategies.

5 Knowing how to learn: the theory

Learning to learn involves learning strategies like planning ahead, monitoring one's performance to identify sources of difficulty, checking, estimating, revision and self testing ... Understanding the strategies of learning and gaining self-knowledge ... helps us to control these processes and give us the opportunity to take responsibility for our own learning.

(Nisbet and Shucksmith 1986: vii)

Introduction

This chapter explores theories of learning. It emphasizes how these can be adopted and adapted by tutors and teachers in helping students to build on their own preferences and strengths to understand their learning. Among other things, consideration is given here to work done on the nature of learning, learning styles and motivation for learning. The importance of teachers' understanding of how such factors influence the success of their teaching methods is a further related issue.

Theories of learning have long engaged the minds of researchers across such diverse fields as educational psychology, sociology and human biology. Thoroughly researched and erudite publications on the nature of knowledge and the processes of learning are sufficient to stock countless shelves in any education library.

The nature of 'intelligence' has also been a fascination for many researchers in trying to understand why some pupils appear to learn more readily and effectively than others. Work by Howard Gardner (1993) has suggested that there are at least eight types of intelligence which should be stimulated, observed and assessed by different means, while Sternberg (1989) argues for a triarchic model of abilities which are important to success in a variety of endeavours. Charles Handy (1997) claims that everyone can lay claim to some form of intelligence, although not always the form that is celebrated in the formal education system and graded in external examinations.

If students do possess different kinds of aptitude, such as those defined by Sternberg and Gardner, it is unlikely that they will all learn in the same way from the same activities. Different students are likely to be more confident and skilled in – and therefore perhaps more motivated to learn from – different sorts of tasks and presentations. This suggests that differences in ability to learn are likely to be a function of students' confidence and skill in internalizing and using information from a particular presentation or task.

Many definitions of learning embracing process and product have been suggested, and the following are but two examples:

> that reflective activity which enables the learner to draw upon previous experience to understand and evaluate the present, so as to shape future action and formulate new knowledge.
>
> (Abbott 1994: viii)

> changes in pupil behaviour as a result of being engaged in an activity or educational experience.
>
> (Kyriacou 1992: 34)

Both these definitions seem appropriate in considering a higher level of learning which includes, for example, analysis, deduction, induction, synthesis and evaluation. We have noted that the aims of many tutoring and action planning activities are to support pupils in understanding and assuming responsibility for the broad skills of learning such as those mentioned above. However, research on learning for the GCSE (Bishop *et al.* 1999), shows that for many teachers and students in Years 10 and 11 (aged 15 or 16), the challenge in learning was still perceived at the level of gaining, retaining and applying of factual subject knowledge. GCSE qualifications were perceived as statements of competence at a basic level of knowledge acquisition. But notwithstanding the best efforts of teachers and lecturers in classroom situations, it is the students themselves who decide whether or not to capture and hold new information. One way of representing our model of the learning process is shown in Figure 5.1.

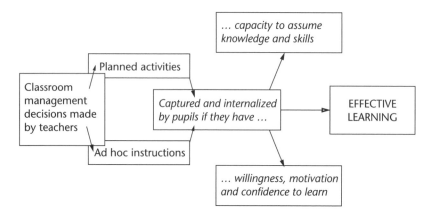

Figure 5.1 *A Model of the Learning Process*

Within our learning model, experiences are multidimensional and students act and react in different ways. The task of the personal tutor is to explore and identify learning experiences and help students understand their own preferences. Most young people appear to be generally accommodating and motivated about the arrangements for learning in formal education. There is a discernible minority, however, for whom learning is not successful, and this group is of continuing concern to teachers, parents and the community in general. Research which can identify and explicate models of teaching that support learning for different students is continuously in demand.

Theories on the nature of learning claim that learning skills and preferences arise from a combination of heredity, past life experiences and socialization. An understanding of the ways in which different people learn, researchers have argued, leads to more appropriate teaching activities and, hence, to better learning. More important, it seems to us, is the simple knowledge that there are infinite, effective ways to learn and that reflection and analysis of one's own preferences are fundamental to a sound understanding of personal strengths and limitations. However, some familiarity with current theories and arguments can only aid tutors and teachers in their support of the learner.

Some theories of learning

Behaviourist approaches

From the beginning of the twentieth century, interest in a systematic and scientific exploration of learning has proliferated. During this time there have been three distinct sets of influence on teaching approaches. The first, between the 1920s and 1950s, was dominated by the behaviourist approaches of psychologists such as Pavlov (1928) and Skinner (1938) who, along with others, demonstrated that animals could be conditioned to respond in new ways to particular stimuli. Reinforcing the desired responses with positive feedback was shown to result in effective learning. These theories are often referred to as stimulus–response (S-R) theories and the practical outcome for schools and teachers was a behavioural-interactionist approach to learning. This gave rise to a technology of instruction (see Rowntree 1974) that searched for the best ways of operating and presenting the curriculum content and then evaluated the most effective learning outcomes. Changes in teaching practice were also advocated. It was claimed that schools habitually operated through a system of punishing unwanted behaviours and a conversion to noticing and rewarding appropriate behaviour was urged (see Wheldall and Glynn 1989).

The long accepted, behaviourist models of Pavlov, Skinner and later Gagné (1975) persuaded a generation of teachers that, with sufficient repetition and reinforcement, children would all respond and learn in a similar way.

Cognitive theory

In the 1950s and 1960s, the work of the Swiss biologist and psychologist Jean Piaget transformed understanding of children's learning. He disagreed with the belief that all learning occurs in response to an externally reinforced stimulus and suggested that the developing child has an innate ability to learn. Piaget famously set out his view that there are four main stages of growth and intellectual development in children, and specified the age limits within which they would occur. Piaget's stages (1971: 126–30) are listed below.

1   *The sensori-motor stage* (up to about 18 or 24 months). In this period intelligent actions are developed in relation to the objects that the baby encounters. These mainly comprise movements and insights without language, but the actions are coordinated in a relatively consistent way. For example, the child can learn to produce pleasing noises by manipulating a musical toy in a certain way.

2   *The pre-operational period* (2 to 7 or 8 years) when actions and objects are grouped, conceptualized and represented by names. However, although it becomes possible to refer to objects, activities and people that are not present perceptually, at this stage the child is still reasoning on the basis of what he or she sees. There is no transformation of reality.

3   *The stage of concrete operations* (between 7 or 8 and 11 or 12 years). Now the child can classify objects according to similarity or difference. He or she can comprehend the conservation of a liquid as it is poured from, for example, a short fat glass to a tall thin one and can visualize other people's perceptions of an object.

4   *The stage of formal logical operations* occurs around the age of 12 when the child becomes capable of reasoning, not only on the basis of objects, but also on the basis of hypotheses or propositions.

These stages are said to be systematic and sequential with each subsequent level of cognitive development, dependent on an interaction between the youngsters' physical and mental interaction with the world around them and the biological maturation of their nervous system. Thus, readiness to learn is linked with children's activities in making sense of new experiences, and their level of maturity in their understanding of the world around them. This was known as cognitive theory as it emphasized the importance of mental development and processing in learning. Piaget put the child at the source of his or her own learning with the teacher merely acting as a provider of experiences and a guide to the reasoning process. One of the weaknesses in this theory was that it gave little emphasis to the accelerating impact of appropriate adult instruction and feedback on both learning and attitude (Lunzer 1989).

In the Piagetian model, students working with personal tutors in secondary schools and colleges would be said to be at the stage of formal operational thinking and would have the ability to use logical reasoning. The majority, therefore, should be well able to reflect on and understand how their own learning occurs, the ways in which they best learn and if and how this differs from their peers.

Social constructivist theories

The third phase in the advance of learning theory in the twentieth century was a focus on learning, not as an accumulation of facts, but as a transformation of pre-existing knowledge. This, it was claimed, emerges from a dis-equilibrium of conflicting experiences that forces the learner into a transformed understanding. According to Ausubel and Robinson (1969: 50–1) the most important factor influencing meaningful learning is not biological development in itself, but the quality, clarity and organization of the learner's present knowledge. New knowledge which cannot be adapted into the framework of the individual cognitive structure, they contend, is 'rote' or acquired by automatic repetition and, as the human mind is not designed to store arbitrary connections, is thus less effective and retainable. The activity of the learner in transforming new material into an appropriate form to augment and extend pre-existing knowledge is the crucial step in learning. Marton and Säljö (1976) develop this concept by distinguishing between the achievements of surface and deep learning.

The belief in a model of information processing was also supported by the work of Jerome Bruner (1971). He defined learning in terms of the formation of concepts and the organization of these concepts into hierarchies, such as those put forward by Bloom (1956) or Gagné (1975). Bruner argued that concepts are neither independent nor discrete, but dynamic changing ideas. Autonomous learning only genuinely results from the effort of discovering and adapting concepts. In his view, it is practice and confidence in working with heuristics by constantly moving from concrete actions to abstract ideas that will enable students, at any age, to develop inquiring minds (Bruner 1971: 122).

Bruner later extended this concept of discovery learning to embrace the work of Vygotsky (1978) who recognized the responsibility of other individuals in sharing culture and consciousness with learners, thus creating what he referred to as the state of dis-equilibrium or disorienting dilemmas. Here he drew on the work of John Dewey (1956) who also pointed out that learning was a social activity. Learning, Dewey argued, is highly dependent on exchanges and contacts with other human beings, teachers, peers and family as well as casual acquaintances. In this way the existing knowledge and capabilities of learners are enhanced and extended, so that in time learners become able to perform at a level they would not have been able to without interaction with another individual or group. Vygotsky called this extending the 'zone of proximal development' (ZPD) while Bruner used the term 'scaffolding' to describe the structured guidance which more informed individuals give to learners to encourage them to develop new skills, attitudes or understanding. We have referred to 'frameworks' constructed by teachers in enabling a student to use such extended tasks to develop higher learning skills such as creativity and critical thinking (see Martin *et al.* 2002). A key to the successful embedding of these high-level skills may be the timely and properly focused removal of the framework.

These social-constructivist theories of learning assert that, in the process of learning, learners construct knowledge and meaning for themselves. The theories emphasize the active, personal nature of learning in contrast to the more passive, behaviourist models which have permeated teacher consciousness for much of the modern era. As Dewey (1956) pointed out, much of traditional education is directed towards isolating students from social interaction, and persuading learners to engage in solitary interactions with materials to be learned. However, Lave and Wenger (1991) contend that learning involves participation in a community of practice. Learning is a process of social participation.

What does this mean for learning?

Theories of learning thus suggest that the acquisition of knowledge is both individual and personal, but also active and social. Independent learning does not mean learning in isolation. Rather, it is the ability to take responsibility for your own learning within the social group (Benson 2001). This means making considered decisions about the purpose and aims of learning, identifying content and gathering information, reflecting and organizing data and evaluating what has been acquired (see also Wallace 2001).

We have had contact with many students who acknowledge that the coursework component of programmes is an activity that helps them understand both the requirements and nature of learning, and themselves as learners (James and Gipps 1998; Bullock *et al.* 2002). Using Ausubel's model (Ausubel and Robinson 1969), this is explained by individuals being able to interact with and develop a topic or activity from their own knowledge base. The flexibility of coursework provides an opportunity for learners to set their own parameters for what they already know and what it is they need to learn, and to consider their preferred way of closing the gap between these two points. Students told us that they learned through coursework because the chosen project was ultimately their responsibility (see also Morgan and Morris 1999):

> Yes, it's actually me doing the thinking. I'm doing it for myself, but they're [the teachers] giving me a helping hand kind of thing ... We had to think for ourselves what was going on, which were good and bad bits and write them down in a plan and put them down in the final coursework.
>
> (Year 10 male student, comprehensive school)

Coursework allowed students to construct their own learning *modus operandi*, agenda and timetables, and this challenge sometimes appeared to have a relevance which was not apparent in other areas of the curriculum. Although they had not heard the terms, many clearly understood that this engagement in their own learning encouraged deep or meaningful learning (Entwhistle 1981; Gipps 1994).

Learning styles

One issue with which teachers have become increasingly familiar is that of the different learning styles of their students. Arguments about the value of categories of cognitive styles and learning strategies persist (Jonassen and Grabowski 1993). Riding and Rayner (1998: 11) describe cognitive style as an individual's preferred and habitual approach to organizing and representing information. Sadler-Smith (2001) points out that the term 'learning styles' is frequently used as an overarching expression for a range of individual constructs including learning preferences, learning strategies, approaches to studying and cognitive styles. In support of this, Riding and Read (1996: 82) point out that: 'in terms of style a person is both good *and* poor at tasks depending on the nature of the task, while for intelligence, they are *either* good *or* poor'.

Different learning styles are nonetheless frequently identified, analysed and contextualized by researchers and writers for the benefit of teachers and learners. Kolb (1984: 41) recognized the influence of experiential learning on our development and saw knowledge as resulting from a combination of 'grasping' and 'transforming' experience. He developed his Learning Styles Inventory to identify preferred modes or styles of learning that ranged along the two bipolar dimensions: the first for grasping experience – 'concrete experience' (CE) to 'abstract conceptualization' (AC) – and the second for transforming that experience into knowledge – 'active experimentation' (AE) to 'reflective observation' (RO). The styles in which individuals prefer to learn, therefore, are determined by their ways of resolving these two dialectics while the idealized learning cycle is portrayed as a spiral where the learner incorporates all the behaviours – experiencing, reflecting, thinking and acting – in a recursive process that responds to the context and content of the learning situation (see Figure 5.2). The ideas of Kolb were pursued by Honey and Mumford (1992) who developed their Learning Styles Questionnaire to identify learners as either activists, theorists, pragmatists or reflectors.

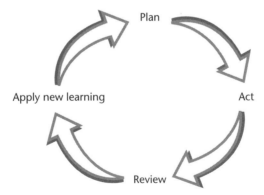

Figure 5.2 *The Learning Cycle*

Similarly, Riding and Rayner (1998) contended that in processing and organizing information individuals tend to be in one of nine types, determined by tendencies towards organizing and processing information in wholes or in parts (the 'wholist-analyst' dimension) and, independently, representing ideas and information through thinking verbally or in mental pictures (the 'verbal-imagery' dimension). Each of the dimensions is a continuum. At the extremes, wholists are 'big picture' people while analytics concentrate on one or two aspects of the situation to the exclusion of the others. Verbalizers think about information in words while imagers create mental pictures, either of representations of the information itself or of associations with it. While learners can fluctuate in their location on the two scales, their position is likely to affect the types of task they will find easy or difficult.

A recent theory that has struck a chord with many teachers has derived from the discipline of neuro-linguistic programming (NLP). This claims that learners prefer to assimilate information by predominantly kinesthetic, audio or visual means (see Dryden and Vos 1994; Smith 1998). According to this theory, 29 per cent of us prefer to learn by seeing and will remember through visualizing pictures, graphs and other scenes and artefacts. A further 34 per cent of us prefer to communicate and learn through sound and interact most successfully with the spoken word, while 37 per cent of learners prefer to engage with the experience physically. The idea of this latter kinesthetic group resonates with Kolb's concept of experiential learning. However, learners in this category are said to be most seriously disadvantaged by the organization and expectations of behaviour in the formal classroom (Smith 1998: 147).

Some researchers have argued that the secret of good learning lies in the skills of the teacher in matching teaching activities with the learning style of the pupil. For example, posters, displays and videos are urged for visual learners; discussion, music and chants for those with an auditory preference; and design, modelling and field trips to engage kinesthetic learners.

A note of caution

Many writers question the trustworthiness of learning style categorizations (e.g. Swailes and Senior 1999; Garner 2000; Duffy and Duffy 2002; Henson and Hwang 2002) and the belief that learning styles should be matched by curricular modifications (Klein 2003). Swailes has argued that analysis of learning styles profiles reveals a dominance of what he calls 'reflector/ theorist' traits. He claims that the four categories of learning style are not supported by the findings, and the observed structure is more indicative of a three-stage learning cycle of action, reflection and planning. Klein also points out that learning styles are usually assessed through a range of perceptions and skills, including cognitive style, which concern central processes such as reasoning and memory. Klein notes that most students indicate mixed and inconsistent preferences for learning styles and he points out that almost all learning activities require different quantities of a variety of skills.

Indeed, categories of learners such as activists, theorists, pragmatists or reflectors, or those preferring kinesthetic or visual messages, are not simple for teachers to recognize. In secondary schools, teachers may only see their pupils for an hour or two each week, not long enough to know them all as individual learners, while pressures of time and equipment often rule out ideals of differentiation. The argument from the identifiers of different learning styles would be that teachers do not need to know the preferred learning styles of their students so long as a variety of teaching strategies are used to match the needs of all learners within the whole class.

A personal tutor can, however, explore such likes and dislikes with his or her tutees. It is important for students to know that not everyone prefers the same methods of learning and that less preferred styles can be identified as areas for development. A sensible comment comes from Joyce *et al.* (1997: 34): 'students are not identical. What helps one person learn a given thing efficiently may not help another so much. Fortunately there are very few known cases where an educational treatment that helps a given type of student a great deal has a serious damaging effect on another type'.

The impact of gender and attainment on learning

On a smaller scale, one of our projects pointed to a notable effect, arising from attainment and gender, on the 28 attitudes to learning which we measured three times over an 18-month time span. In 9 of the 26 sample schools, the boys responded more positively to the attitude statements, and in 5 schools the girls were clearly more positive. In all schools, lower attaining students were more positive to the impact of a one-to-one discussion with their tutor than the higher attaining group. That gender and prior achievement have an influence on how pupils see themselves as learners is well supported by other research (see Elwood 1995; MacGilchrist *et al.* 1997).

In our study, potential reasons for the gender effect such as organizational issues, the predominant gender of the tutor team, the impact of other initiatives in the school and the socioeconomic status of the students were sought from the schools. No common factors were found and the most recurring explanation for the observation was the strong influence of particular friendship groups of boys or girls in a particular year (see Lave and Wenger 1991). However, tutors agreed that pupils who had less opportunity for self-focused, one-to-one conversations with an informed adult out of school benefited more than others from the dialogue with their tutor. This group is likely to comprise lower achieving males and this effect may also be linked to the socioeconomic status and culture of the family (Bernstein 1988).

While it seems that preferred learning style is independent of gender and ability, our research has identified four groups from a gender and perceived ability matrix: high ability girls, high ability boys, low ability girls and low ability boys show different characteristics relating to measures of confidence and skill (see also Riding and Read 1996). The generalities which were suggested by our research were that high ability boys are most positive and confident about their own knowledge of their skills and abilities; high ability girls are most willing and comfortable in conversation with adults and peers; while low ability students (and boys in particular) benefit most (in relative terms) from one-to-one discussion with their teachers and from activities which help them plan their short- and long-term targets. These characteristics may be more potent than preferred learning style, and are certainly more obvious for teachers.

Recently, Morgan and Morris (1999: 64) found that, whatever their age and ability, boys and girls have similar priorities regarding the management of pedagogy. Both genders also agreed that one of the most important factors in successful lessons is a variety of methods of presentation.

In a time of concern over low achieving boys, both finding and funding the time to listen to their experiences and concerns and to discuss strategies for learning may be worth wider consideration. While gender is a clear and immutable variable, prior attainment can be measured in different ways (Sternberg 1988; Gardner 1993). How this is internalized and accepted by individual students may have an important impact on subsequent effort and achievement. Discussion with a teacher or tutor can boost confidence and help to provide realistic expectations of success.

Talking about learning

The ability to communicate through talk is a type of intelligence (Sternberg 1988; Gardner 1993) which is easily recognized, but within the classroom this can be constrained to particular situations and formats. The benefits of all students having a separate timetabled slot to talk to tutors about forms of knowledge and culture in relation to their own learning strengths and weaknesses are only now being recognized.

According to Vygotsky (1986), language is the most important of the psychological tools that shape our thinking, feelings and behaviours; and it has been acknowledged that good communication about work motivates learners (Harris and Bell 1986). Bruner (1971: 107) contributed to this belief with his thoughts that: 'one of the most crucial ways in which a culture provides aid in intellectual growth is through a dialogue between the more experienced and less experienced, providing a means for the internalization of dialogue in thought. The courtesy of dialogue may be the major ingredient in the courtesy of teaching'.

In their research into the benefits of pupil talk, Rudduck *et al.* (1996) state that relationships at school are an important influence affecting pupils' attitudes to their learning. They note that it was apparent that pupils valued the teacher-pupil relationship particularly when teachers were available to talk to pupils about learning and schoolwork. We repeat the quote, also used in Chapter 3, from Claxton (1990: 107) who stresses the importance of talk as a strategy for learning: 'If you can talk to your teachers, or your Mum and Dad or, most importantly, your friends about school work you may be in a more powerful position than those who cannot'. The benefit of such teacher-student talk is that it is, at least partly, in the control of the pupil. Most classroom discourse is at the invitation of the teacher (see Norman 1992) and conducted in an open forum. Activities, such as personal development (or learning) planning put pupils in a different relationship with their tutors, and remove the distraction or influence of the peer group. There are clearly two strands to this strategy of dialogue with an informed adult: exercising the ability to articulate what is known in order to meet the requirements of tests and examinations; and developing an understanding of how the pupil, as an individual, learns best. If talk is to be a successful tool for learning it needs to be well structured and focused on these components without diminishing the element of pupil control. This is neither a simple, nor necessarily a natural, task for tutors.

The action planning initiatives we observed were welcomed by tutors, often more than by students themselves, for the level of insight they provided about their students' perceptions, experiences and difficulties. In the most propitious cases, such insights allowed teachers more accuracy and confidence in providing the appropriate scaffolding for individual students' planning for learning. Similarly, the process of generating a personal plan with the help of their tutor or an informed adult helped some young people understand the steps for accomplishing better learning. In the most successful cases, the one-to-one dialogue helped them to understand the diverse and continuous nature of human understanding and to identify specific activities which would enable them to learn. As one articulate pupil explained: 'It [the one-to-one dialogue] gets you thinking about the type of person you are. What your skills and abilities are, what you want to be and what you can do about it' (Year 11 student, comprehensive school).

Motivations for learning

Returning to our diagram at the beginning of this chapter (Figure 5.1), an understanding of the processes of learning does not necessarily explain the influences which affect some young people and not others. Two of the most pressing influences on students, as they approach critical stages in their educational experiences, are their relationships with their peers and the looming necessity of external examinations. The motivations and emotions which are stirred by these can have a significant impact on learning. As all teachers and educators know, the differential psychology of individuals has a fundamental impact on the processes of learning, and the personality of the learner is likely to be even more crucial than the teaching skills of the educator.

The findings of Rudduck *et al.* (1996) have supported our own finding (Bullock and Wikeley 1999) of the existence of this rhetorical desire to succeed, but it is clearly not always the reality of what teachers routinely encounter in the classroom. Young people, at heart, want to do well and are prepared to work hard to do so; but for some there is a barrier between their espoused desires and their practical achievement. For certain pupils the processes and practices entailed in 'working hard' may need to be explicitly discussed and set out in repeated explications.

That personal motivation is a key to learning is not in doubt. It has been argued (Rowntree 1988; Jonassen and Grabowski 1993) that motivation can arise either from the need to succeed or from the need to avoid failure. Others have argued that motivation is a function of current incentive and conditioned need (Graham and Weiner 1996). Dweck (2000) notes that there is no clear relationship between students' abilities and their motivation. She identified the level of pupils' understanding of procedures for rising to a challenge and coping with failure as underpinning a mastery-oriented mindset. However, a mastery orientation will help students become more able over time and a weakness in this area may build a barrier between the rhetoric and reality of pupil achievement.

Goleman (in MacGilchrist *et al.* 1997: 108) argues that emotional intelligence is another vital capacity for learning. Emotional intelligence can be described as having an understanding of motivation and a capacity for persistence, control of impulse, regulation of mood and the ability to keep distress from swamping the ability to think. It has some overlaps with the new '3Rs' (readiness, resilience, reflection) suggested by Claxton (1996) as the requisites for learning. Additionally, Salovery and Mayer (also in MacGilchrist *et al.* 1997) have summarized self-awareness, managing emotions, motivating oneself, recognizing emotions in others and handling relationships as vital to emotional intelligence.

The centrality of reflection

It has been claimed (Schön 1983; Boud *et al.* 1985) that personal reflection is the key to transforming learning from the mechanistic accumulation of facts to the higher order, creative processes of applying knowledge to new situations and to solving problems. Schön argued that there is a difference between theories in use, or what we routinely and instinctively do, and espoused theories – what we say we do and what we would like others to think that we do. Reflection on activities, tasks and experiences enables tacit knowledge to become explicit and the gap between theories in use and espoused theories to be recognized. Thus the goals and processes of learning become better understood and more effective. Reflection allows new thinking to be accommodated into existing learning and beliefs, and the whole to be adjusted. Schön and his colleague Chris Argyris (1974) called this 'double loop learning' in preference to 'single loop learning' which may be realized without plans, values or targets being questioned. Reflection is an ongoing process. Priorities and options change and we need to continually reflect on and highlight what is important to us.

Boud and Walker (1998) point out that reflection is not always accommodated within a higher education setting. How much less likely is it to be achieved in a school classroom? Young people who are being helped to realize the impact of personal reflection on their learning need support in small social friendship groups or a one-to-one situation. Reflection often occurs most effectively in combination with, or as a result of, dialogue with other people. Broadfoot (1997) argues that reflection and discussion between student and teacher support the learning process as well as improving motivation. A reflective cycle (see Figure 5.3) that might underpin the interactions between the personal tutor and their students has been adapted from the work of Donald Schön and others.

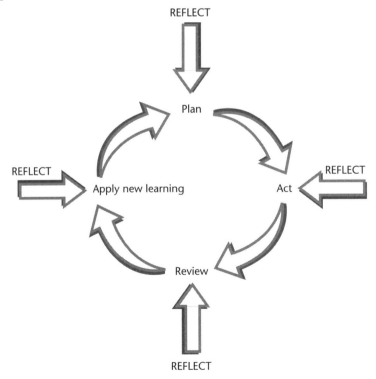

Figure 5.3 *The Reflective Cycle*

In the school or college setting the cycle relates to the focus of formal instruction. Reflection means active rationalization and reconstruction by making connections between input information and the information already stored in memory, or basic intuitive self-awareness that results from the bio-functioning of the body. The role for the tutor therefore becomes one of facilitating that reflection through the careful use of probing, reflexive questions: 'Personal decision making is examining your actions and knowing their consequences ... and taking responsibility for the actions' (Goleman 1997: 303).

Tutors should focus the reflection on students' efforts and not on their abilities. Many students assume that effort is required only by the less able. They have not yet come to the realization that sustained effort over time is the key to achievement.

Conclusions

Reflection on our own work suggests that there are some fundamental truths about learning that many students (and some teachers) fail to appreciate. Explicit information, guidance and practice relating to these would make young people's understanding of how to learn more obvious. While this must be a task for all teachers and educators, it is a priority for those who have responsibilities as personal tutors. For example, our research pointed to three main issues:

- Students need to know that learning is *active* rather than passive, but that the same activities are not necessarily equally effective for all people.
- Students also need to know that the ability to learn is dependent on a range of information gathering and processing *skills*, such as collecting and organizing data and identifying and reforming concepts, and that proficiency in these skills is not innate. Once the skill is recognized as a mechanism for learning, it can be refined and practised (Cooper and McIntyre 1996).
- Finally, students need to know that learning is *social*. Interaction with and feedback from more capable others (and also peers) are a formative and powerful source of learning.

These points are often not made clear nor accommodated in schools and colleges (see also James and Gipps 1998). This occurs despite a legacy of writings on models of learning in which seminal thinkers have emphasized the notion of active learning, the benefits of practising the activity and the formative influence of social groups. Considerations of theories and styles of learning suggest that there should be an entitlement for all students in secondary school and beyond to at least an annual one-to-one conversation with a mentor or tutor. The provision of such facilities from Year 7, or even as early as Key Stage 2, might well be cost effective in the long term. In this dialogue it needs to be stressed that all individuals are able to learn to learn, and that talking about the nature and process of learning is beneficial for learning activities.

Our studies also point to different attitudes and responses to learning in males and females and high and low attaining pupils (see also MacGilchrist *et al.* 1997). A consideration of teaching and learning strategies which meet the needs of these particular groups could be very helpful in ensuring more effective learning for all. When planning professional development for teachers and tutors, a shared view of learning might be fostered if the processes of learning to learn and the impact that teachers are able to make in supporting their pupils' learning were emphasized more explicitly.

If to be successful, schools and teachers need to manage and support aspects of emotional intelligence and social interaction as well as imparting subject knowledge, then different strategies must be available. It is almost impossible to imagine that whole-class techniques can be effective in promoting emotional intelligence. Encouraging pupils to assume responsibility for their own work, either singly or in small supportive groups, and providing strategies to manage this, will contribute towards raised emotional intelligence; while time to talk on a one-to-one, adult-pupil basis is paramount in focusing and valuing effort. The *Standards for Qualified Teacher Status* (Teacher Training Agency 2002: 10) state that those to be awarded such status must demonstrate that they give: 'immediate and constructive feedback to support pupils as they learn. They involve pupils in reflecting on, evaluating and improving their own performance'. This lip-service to the benefits derived from one-to-one and small-group work can only be transformed into a reality with greater consideration among policy-makers, teacher educators and practitioners to strategies for establishing the resources and teacher skills for one-to-one student-tutor learning experiences.

As we enter the twenty-first century, there is still tension between concern for students as individual learners and the necessary formal systems and structures of institutions of learning. One way that schools and colleges are reconciling the tension is through the work of personal tutors with dedicated time for one-to-one discussions with their tutees. This provides time to revisit and test out ideas with a more experienced other. Furthermore, it addresses students' need for support through good quality relationships with an informed adult (see Gray and Wilcox 1995: MacBeath *et al.* 1996) to ensure that each student finds, and understands, his or her own preferred path through the learning maze.

6 Helping students develop skills for learning

Female 1:   *If you think about your learning you have to think about what you do. Like when it comes to revision and everything you focus more on the subject, to learn more in it. I think it would help you in the future because you've got to do that in a job as well.*

Female 2:   *Yes. If you haven't thought about it, then you've got loads of different ways to go, but if you think about it then you've got one line to go along and you can focus your ideas.*

(Year 9 students, comprehensive school)

Introduction

The lesson to be learned from the previous chapter is that learning is a complicated and complex activity. It can be approached in a myriad of ways and no one way will be successful for all individuals, or even for any individual in all circumstances. Learning is often unexpected and unplanned, which is perhaps a timely lesson for those aiming to facilitate and support young people's development. However, learning is the purpose of schools and colleges, and this chapter illustrates how some have considered ways of helping their students develop the skills and strategies described in Chapter 5. Of course this cannot be done in isolation. Which skills and strategies need to be deployed in particular situations depends on what is being learned (see Chapters 7 and 8), and by whom it is being learned (see Chapters 3 and 4). In working with schools and colleges, we have identified some strategies that personal tutors (and class teachers) use to facilitate learning. Their purpose is to help students understand the fundamental truths of learning described in Chapter 5:

- learning is often a *social* process;
- learning involves *information gathering* and *processing skills*; and
- learning is *active*.

As set out in Figure 5.3 in the previous chapter, learning usually occurs in stages and these are each enhanced and consolidated by *reflection*.

The social dimension of learning

We have become convinced of the importance of the social aspect of learning. In all the research we have conducted with students and teachers, rarely have we met any students who do not refer to talking about their learning with teachers, checking out their understanding with peers or discussing their futures with family and friends. While there is some support for the notion that higher ability students are more likely to be able to discuss and formulate their plans with other adults outside the school setting, the tutorial process itself appears to have a notable impact with lower attaining groups.

Some institutions experienced benefits in starting the personal tutorial process with group discussions (friendship groups) sharing what the students were currently doing in and out of school and identifying successes and weaknesses. Tutors thought that this provided a foundation for (and hence improved) the later one-to-one discussions. Students felt that group interviews with friends made for better discussions, as their perceptions of each other helped identify individual strengths and skills. They saw the group interviews as being about identifying key skills, but the individual interviews were necessary for setting personal targets and writing the action planning document. Considerations of time and need were required to decide whether a preliminary small group consultation was held. One teacher felt strongly that holding a class discussion, so that relevant arguments and theories could be shared, was beneficial for all. Several agreed that this is particularly powerful in a mixed ability group and some also stressed the value of mixing abilities for small-group work:

> Mixed ability teaching does help with that. If we were setted, bottom set students would never see the creative ideas that the B and A and A* [high attaining] students were coming out with. By teaching mixed ability you open everyone up to those ideas. Also remembering that some D/E [low attaining] candidates are superb orally. They'll come out with fantastic ideas, which perhaps no one else does.
>
> (English teacher, comprehensive school)

Information gathering and processing

As we have already pointed out, a major finding from our research and that of others is the positive impact of one-to-one dialogues between students and personal tutors. We have argued that for greatest effectiveness the dialogues should clearly focus on individual learning and should explore simple strategies for effective learning with students. Personal tutors may find it useful to consider whether these aims could be more clearly emphasized in one-to-one sessions, or perhaps explored in preliminary group work. This may involve some analysis of the nature of a particular task or clarification of what constitutes criteria for success. It is likely that, with benefits from their own reflections and ongoing experiences, the activity of listening to students' understandings and perceptions will enable tutors to support their students' learning more effectively.

In Chapters 3 and 4 we discussed the importance of giving feedback in one-to-one tutorials in order to help students reflect on themselves as learners. Here we address the strategies that might be used to trigger and focus this reflection. For example, we think, not only about the specific skills and requirements needed in order to meet the criteria for tests and examinations, but also about the metacognitive strategies associated with high attainment and knowing how to learn. Such strategies are useful if they help students to understand something, act more effectively or achieve a goal. The same strategies will not work for all, but must be considered and evaluated by each individual in terms of their efficacy. Information gathering and processing skills can be grouped into key areas.

First, students need to explore thinking skills – what they are and how they can be used. There are many conceptualizations of thinking skills and there are countless publications that exemplify these and suggest how they may be engendered. Despite some claims, however, there is no holy grail, and no best way of teaching thinking skills. It can be valuable for students and their tutors to consider and select the most appropriate cognitive strategy for a task. The kind of thinking skills that might be useful include:

- retrieving information;
- comparing and contrasting ideas;
- identifying issues and relationships;
- developing an argument;
- making judgements;
- decision making;
- problem solving; and so on.

These are skills that are frequently discussed in group and one-to-one tutorials. Guidance on gathering, organizing and using information from the library, from the internet and from people with appropriate knowledge is a common topic in tutorial time. Skills for recognizing similarities and differences in concepts and sets of information, and extracting meaning from information in order to develop an argument or make judgements are fundamental, but are usually addressed in subject areas. Students should know that these are transferable skills that can be identified and applied to different contexts. Time in tutorials can be well spent by identifying a transdisciplinary skill, reflecting on where and how in the curriculum it has already been used, and considering whether or not it could be useful in a different situation.

Second, students need to consider what is meant by quality in any particular context and decide how this can be evidenced and demonstrated. Some questions that could be discussed by the personal tutor and their tutees include the following:

- What is the evidence that students can use to support their conclusions in any review of their work and achievements?
- How can students evaluate their own achievements sensibly and honestly?
- What constitutes the criteria for success in any task?
- How do we know a piece of work is good?
- How could a piece of work be improved?
- How can we learn from assessment?

While these skills may be difficult for many students to achieve explicitly (although there may be some who are 'within sight' of demonstrating such skills), they can be addressed implicitly by, for example, peer assessment or by assessing exemplars using assessment criteria. The formative dimensions to students' experience of teaching and learning are thus increased (as suggested in Chapter 3) with the tutor being in a good position to facilitate reflection. Schools, colleges and individual teachers could benefit from developing appropriate opportunities for such student self-assessment.

Tutors also need to be aware of the skills underpinning the ability to communicate clearly with students about formative assessment. For example, rather than asking generally 'What do you want to improve?', tutors need to help students identify where their weaknesses lie, what they can feasibly improve and how they are going to get there:

They tend to say, 'I must improve my homework/do better in class/those sorts of things, unless you pin them down and say, 'What's your weakest subject? Maths – well what can you do to improve that?' and then they start to think about very specific subject linked things, but we go woolly if we have wide questions.

(Year 9 tutor, comprehensive school)

Analysis of students' attitudes to writing coursework (Bishop *et al.* 2003) suggests that different students, according to their ability, require quite different levels of feedback, if the teacher is to enable the student to improve his or her learning. Developing students' critical faculties, and thus enhancing their skills as decision makers, is crucial. In other words, helping students to make critical judgements about the validity (and hence quality) of their work requires attention to analytical thought and an understanding of the processes of students' learning on the part of the teacher. And of course the student needs time to come to terms with the implications of developing reflective approaches to coursework. Clearly, there is a need and an opportunity to re-orientate feedback towards developing students' learning – for example, in relation to thinking skills – and for this to be for all students and not simply those who are 'within sight' of demonstrating such skills. There is something to be said for helping students to become aware of their thinking about thinking (whatever their current level of reasoning) as a tool in the scaffolding process, rather than simply aiming at the top level students because that is the level at which it will be *explicitly* evidenced. Tutors thus have a key role in developing *appropriate formative feedback*.

For lower ability students, however, lack of observable critical and evaluative skills was also contingent on a more fundamental difficulty in expressing investigations and findings in writing:

> I might give them several suggestions and pull several suggestions out of them – 'How might you go about doing this?' and then writing the suggestions down. So it might be ways in which they can present work, things they can do with data. They have particular problems with conclusions and evaluations and they also have problems – they can pick out that field number one had the most litter in it, but quite often they find it difficult to see that it's because field number one was next to the car park. So it's trying to prompt those things out of them. It's those elements that get them the highest marks.
>
> (Geography teacher, comprehensive school)

Finally it must be clear how 'thinking about thinking' can enhance students' work. There is a need for reflective and sensible thinking that is focused on what to believe or what to do. Skills of reflection are honed by a clear purpose with an aim of uncovering 'What did I do well?', 'Where were the weaknesses?' and 'How can I improve?'

We found that students, working at the whole-class or at the individual level, often associated critical thinking with high stress situations. Teacher-student interactions that monitor the production of pieces of work were often seen to be situations where the 'cards are stacked' in the teacher's favour and were perceived by students as confrontations and apparent challenges to their individuality and identity. Challenging comfortable mental habits undoubtedly involves risk for the learner.

Away from the stresses of subject knowledge, the personal tutor can provide an opportunity to make the connections between specific subject-oriented learning and the more general learning skills students have already developed, but may not have recognized. Tutorial questions need to be formulated at a higher-order level in order to make those connections explicit (Morgan and Saxton 1991), otherwise the exercise becomes mechanistic and its real purpose is not understood by the students. Examples might include:

- How would you explain ... ?
- What if this or that was the case? What then?
- How can you justify ... ?
- Why do you think ... ?
- ... and so on.

A simple ploy in engaging with these types of question was shared with us by a personal tutor. This was to increase the 'wait time' for student responses, and provided a dual benefit in both giving time for the student to take control of the dialogue and in allowing a deeper and more considered response.

Setting targets and objectives

The one-to-one or small-group sessions with the personal tutor acted as an additional forum for discussing strategies for information gathering and processing. Guidance for this was, of course, primarily set out in the subject lessons, but the opportunity for clarification and confirmation from the personal tutor allowed students a greater sense of confidence and purpose. The personal dialogue resulted in an action plan, normally written on a prepared pro forma by the pupil, which set out clear targets or objectives together with appropriate actions and times to achieve them by.

Target setting is a key issue for schools, and not just because it is part of government policy which is impacting greatly on schools and colleges at the current time. In recent years, schools and colleges have been directed to set their own targets for expected successes in external examinations. This has involved greater scrutiny of the quantitative data generated by the institution, usually in terms of test or examination scores. Test scores of year groups have been analysed to explore trends across gender, subject departments, socioeconomic group and the like. Many schools have become data rich with such analyses, but not all have decided on the best ways to use the information. One school we are working with has plotted students' non-verbal scores in standardized tests against their verbal scores (see Figure 6.1). An observation is that there is a group of students whose verbal score is lower than their non-verbal score. The school is concerned that these students are not achieving their full potential and is seeking a change in teaching approach or activity that would remedy this. For example, setting this group more challenging targets. Some reflection by the personal tutor with each member of this group about their engagement with learning may also be fruitful. Another solution would involve a discussion (either small group or one-to-one) between the tutor and the class members to explore the motivations and interests of each individual in order to highlight barriers to learning and consider how to overcome these.

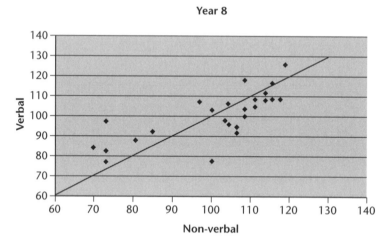

Figure 6.1 *Plot of Cognitive Abilities Test (CAT) non-verbal scores against verbal scores*

There has been much discussion about how to construct a good target (Ofsted 1996; Flecknoe 2001; Martinez 2001c). Part of the learning process for tutors is therefore the understanding that targets have to be specific and achievable in the short term and discussion in tutorials needs to be structured in order to help students reflect on specific actions. The acronym SMART (specific, measurable, achievable, relevant and timed) has been used to help tutors and mentors work with their students in developing sound targets. The following SMART approach and guidance to setting targets is commonly provided for students:

- Be *specific* – the target must state clearly what you are committing to and should identify what will be different when the target has been achieved.

- Make targets *measurable* so that you and your tutor will be able to tell if you are meeting them.
- Your targets should be challenging and require significant action so that you must stretch yourself to complete them, but they must be *achievable* because, if targets are too difficult, you will never feel a sense of progression or success.
- Targets must feed in and be *relevant* to your personal learning agenda.
- Include a specific *time*/date for completion of significant stages.

SMART targets are identified by the student after consideration and discussion with his or her personal tutor about personal goals and achievements. Evidence used to focus this discussion is related to personal and social development, school activities and work and expectations beyond school. It can include:

- grades and marks;
- other monitoring data (merits, attendance, lateness, behaviour etc.);
- teacher ongoing assessments;
- student self assessments;
- out of school achievements.

In almost all our research, these topics underpin the substantive content of one-to-one sessions between a student and his or her personal tutor, and inform the two or three targets that are set for a coming time span. Tutors also ensure that students have the practical knowledge to help them meet targets. For example, they discuss sources of information such as careers libraries, books, the internet and so on and sometimes, when necessary, refer students to other teachers or adults who can offer advice. In many schools and colleges, the systems for obtaining informal support from other teachers and adults were often not well established and this is perhaps an area that needs to be addressed by senior managers, teachers and tutors.

However, the emphasis on target setting that has been at the heart of government policymaking in recent years leads to a note of caution. The perceived stress on targets has appeared to encourage the misconception that setting targets is equivalent to learning. Our research highlighted the extent and folly of this idea. Many students have come to regard a target as a task for completion. However, they may or may not achieve it and may or may not learn from it. In general terms, students have not been encouraged to consider the relationship between targets and learning (see also the section above) nor have they identified the generic learning skills that could be practised in achieving a target. A key idea that students need to understand is that a target represents a step towards a learning goal. Target setting and learning are both active and reflective. In our experience there is very little discussion in schools and colleges as to why targets are a useful tool for learning, and many students and tutors are overwhelmed by what they perceive as target overload: 'You are just getting ready for the summer holiday and they give you more targets!' (Year 10 female student, comprehensive school).

Capturing the action plan

Planning is a necessary stage in learning. In learning about learning it can be helpful to consider how plans can be made definite and structured, so that they become more than vague intentions. In most of the personal tutoring projects we have encountered, a plan written either by hand or electronically was the main outcome from the one-to-one discussion. This act of writing had the benefits of producing concrete evidence of intentions and allowing some reflection on the task identified. However, a lack of enthusiasm in writing down personal plans and targets has been consistently observed in action planning initiatives (Broadfoot *et al.* 1988; Bullock and Jamieson 1995; Bullock and Wikeley 1999; see also our argument in Chapter 4):

> They're difficult to write in words.
>
> I think PLPs should spend more time on important things instead of writing a paper.
>
> (Year 9 students, comprehensive school)

The research suggests that the negativity about recording is not particularly related to age, but neither is it common to all institutions. Personal tutors are well aware of these sentiments and many have designed appropriate strategies to respond to them. These have included:

- making joint notes or using audiotapes during discussions which students later used to write up their plan;
- using word processing packages; and
- earmarking ten minutes after each individual interview for pupils to sit quietly and comfortably on their own, reflecting on their discussion with the tutor, and writing a rough draft of their plan which at a later stage was written out more carefully on the designated pro forma.

Help in capturing ideas and structuring thinking was offered by a number of tutors to ensure that evidence for reflection was not lost because of a disinclination to record in writing:

> What I then tend to do is talk it through with them and write down for them any points we've raised and discussed. So they may come up with the answer, but I act as a scribe in fact and write those ideas down for them so that they've got a log and a record, because after a conversation they forget. I also think as staff we sometimes forget they're not just doing our subject, they're doing many others.
>
> (Year 9 tutor, comprehensive school)

However, in enhancing learning, there is a balance to be maintained between helping pupils capture their learning plans comfortably and legibly, and allowing them to have ownership of the document (see Pole 1993). A sense of ownership is crucial if learning is to be an active process. In this day and age, when much of what happens in schools is prescribed by the government, and when the gaining of accredited qualifications involves such high stakes, it is easy for young people to see learning as something that is given to them or even imposed upon them. School is a detached experience that many students endure because they have to. That is not to say they necessarily dislike it (although some do) or even object to being there, but few have any sense of ownership. If students retain a sense of detachment from the whole learning process then they are unlikely to take responsibility for it.

Student ownership implies that the use, style and content of the written plan is within *their* authority. Ownership by the school implies constraints of use, standards and presentation. Interviews and document scrutiny in the PLP study showed that some schools used the plan in Year 9 as a presentation document which is sent home to parents and that there was an almost universal tutor anticipation that it would be used in Year 10 as a basis for discussion leading to the Record of Achievement. While these expectations undoubtedly raised the profile and importance of the plan, they may simultaneously have contributed to pupils' perceptions of it as a school-owned product and school-directed process.

The bottom line in this tension may be that it is very difficult for schools and tutors not to put some stress on the presentation of a final document which will undoubtedly be seen by parents and others, and hence may be judged as a reflection of effective teaching or tutoring. Tutors may also believe that students' perceptions of the value of a document which is not encouraged to be presented to acceptable standards is likely to be minimal. Whether or not this is the price of true student ownership, and whether or not it can be paid, may need to be debated within institutions.

Where the tutorial file is kept and who has access to it are, therefore, fundamental issues. If students are to truly believe that they are active players in the learning process then having access to records of their learning, and the opportunity to contribute to them, is vital. Files can be hard copy, located in secure cabinets in the tutor room or tutor's office, or can be electronic with access by password. The range of records and documentation in the tutor file can include tutor reviews, subject reviews, attendance and achievement data, records of interviews, action plans, review documents and records of any interviews or telephone calls to parents (Martinez 2001c).

Nonetheless, student-controlled recording systems will always be seen as merely tokenistic if the power relationships in all other aspects of the institution are firmly weighted in favour of the teaching staff. In all the schools and colleges we have worked with, the one-to-one interviews were described by the tutors as student-led, whereas this was not always the students' view. Many saw the whole process as controlled by the tutor. The tutors asked the questions, and sometimes took the notes that the students then wrote up 'in neat'. There often seemed to be some student confusion about the reason for the document, apart from a vague understanding that it might help them achieve what they wanted to do in the future: 'I think you bring it back in Y10. I am not sure why' (Year 9 student, comprehensive school). Others highlighted their sense of detachment from the whole learning process. When asked if they thought the PLP process would help them learn they replied: 'I don't think it will because all it's about is yourself and your exams aren't about yourself' (Year 9 student, comprehensive school).

Completing the circle – the follow up

Our research and that of others (Rudduck *et al.* 1996; Duffield *et al.* 2000) makes clear that the great majority of students are well motivated by the desire to succeed at school and in their future choices. However, most were not able to, or did not know how to, turn this motivation into action. The evaluation of PLP (Bullock and Wikeley 1999) showed, as might be expected, that it had a positive effect on pupils' knowledge about how and where to get information to help them with their future planning. However, it also showed that there is a difference between the intentions of setting targets and the reality of achieving them, and for some students there was a difficulty in moving from the relatively simple intention represented by planning to the appropriate actions of carrying out the task. There is a gap between the ability to set targets and the ability to achieve them. As one Year 9 girl observed: 'Although you talk to your tutor about what you want to do, there's not a lot of guidance about how to achieve it' (Year 9 student, comprehensive school).

An effective action planning cycle does not stop when plans are written and targets are set. Learners need encouragement and interest at each stage of the cycle. The aim, therefore, is not linking current work to long-term targets but breaking down shorter-term targets into recognizable steps of achievement: 'I think the life plan, the long term, whether they want to live in a city or in the country is irrelevant really. I think perhaps, it is better that they concentrate on the way they're learning and the targets that help them focus on that' (tutor, comprehensive school).

An issue that exercised institutions was the completion of the circle in acknowledging and celebrating the targets that had been met. Tutors recognized the imperative for this in consolidating a sense of worth among students in relation to the target-setting process and the personal tutorial system. The marking of success also acts to generate motivation; a truth observed by Flecknoe (2001: 222) in his comment: 'the setting and achieving of targets, previously just out of our reach is a necessary condition for us to feel happy'. However, in schools and colleges with limited time for one-to-one discussions, such opportunities are rarely built into the system, and completion of targets has not been explicitly emphasized. While some colleges were able to integrate regular one-to-one slots between student and tutor so that individual progress was continually monitored, and the achievement (or not) of targets discussed, in other institutions opportunities to celebrate successful target completion were intermittent or redundant.

One school we encountered, however, did have an effective arrangement where pupils set academic and personal targets in their one-to-one discussion and then selected a subject teacher or other adult to monitor them and indicate when targets were achieved. This had the effect of involving more staff in target setting and encouraging the individual pupil to ensure that the target was met by an agreed date.

In one special school, subject targets were set with the subject teacher before being discussed as part of the learning plan with the personal tutor. The subject teachers then had the responsibility of monitoring progress with the student. The smaller teaching classes in special education obviously makes this approach more practical:

'but it's actually the responsibility of the person setting the target to review it with the student. The tutor will acknowledge their awareness and maybe comment on it, but the actual responsibility of saying "Have you met this target and should we now change it?" is theirs'
(PLP coordinator, moderate learning difficulty school).

But the main complaint from tutors was the lack of time to review and revisit targets and therefore help students to move on. Unless this happened the targets became meaningless and far from acting as a motivating factor became demotivating. Targets should not be about accountability but about breaking learning into discrete achievable chunks that can promote progress by enhancing the learner's sense of success. There is a danger, observed in some of the schools we have worked with, that the setting of the target becomes the metaphor for learning. In some schools, when we asked about learning, the staff would immediately talk about target setting instead. But often no more thought was given to a target until it was achieved, and sometimes not even then. A target is only useful if it is accompanied by a discussion of exactly the steps needed to achieve it. A target is only useful if the achievement of it reveals the next step in the learning process. That is why it is so personal to the individual – one student's understanding of how to get from 'here' to 'there' will be very different from that of another, even when 'here' and 'there' are exactly the same points. This point was made most clearly from our work with special schools, because in special schools all learning tends to be explicit and therefore easier to see, but we would strongly argue that it applies equally to those working in mainstream schools and colleges.

Whatever the systems selected, it is important to embed recognized systems for acknowledging the completion of short-term targets into the process. The setting of targets is not sufficient in itself. It is having the commitment, skills and ability to achieve them that will allow students to become lifelong learners. For that to happen, the circle must be complete.

Conclusions

In one of our PLP schools the coordinator described the action planning process as being about improving students' learning capabilities, and we would agree with this view. For some schools, however, personal tutoring is still viewed as an opportunity to interact with, and get to know, students at a more informal level. Although this is helpful, it leaves students with the perception that the dialogue is primarily a school requirement for making option choices. Such gaps in perception have been recorded in other studies (e.g. Morgan and Morris 1999). While both parties appear to enjoy the one-to-one experience, it seems that neither makes the most of the process, and students are not able to make the links with learning about learning. Tutors discover interesting information about their students but, in general, miss the opportunity to explore the dynamics of individual pupil learning. A one-to-one discussion with students is clearly a learning opportunity for teachers, as well as students, and needs to be heralded as such. However, in general, there needs to be more discussion between teachers and individual students about the ways in which learners can be supported to understand the nature of knowledge and learning, and how they can be encouraged how to think rather than be taught what to think. Schools wishing to make the most of such opportunities need to think about:

- the nature and influence of structured teacher-student dialogues;
- the processes of target setting and the use of student-level data among other sources of information; and
- the provision of subsequent support for achieving targets.

The relationship between tutor and pupil is clearly a crucial factor in effective learning. Our research has shown that students value a positive climate in their tutorial sessions and this is characterized by challenging but realistic expectations, warmth and encouragement, and pleasant physical surroundings.

The tutor, however, is only one of many subject teachers and the personal tutorial dialogue is only the first step to improved learning in school. Simple strategies for sharing information and targets arising from tutorials need to be considered by schools in order to develop this link with effective learning. The fundamental notion of how teachers and students communicate about learning should be a focus for staff discussion and professional development throughout the school. The importance of all teachers overtly modelling their own learning processes and strategies cannot be overstressed.

7 Knowing what to learn: the theory

The school should enable ... a sense of connection between the learner and the natural environment, learner and social responsibility, learner and work, learner and learning, learner and the sense of self.

(Clarke 2000: 9)

Introduction

In most of the developed world, the law obliges children between specified ages to be formally educated. In the United Kingdom, education is compulsory between the ages of 5 and 16. Other countries prefer to delay the required start of education for a year, or even two. Most children attend school for their compulsory education, with only a very few making other arrangements. Between the ages of 16 and 19 those young people in the UK who wish to continue their formal education (the majority) have the choice of remaining in the school system or transferring into the further education sector. This latter sector is covered by specific legislation relating to adult and further education, and the statutory obligation for provision lies mainly with the Further Education Funding Council.

The aim of this chapter is to explore the rationale and principles underpinning the bodies of knowledge, the plans and the experiences that compose the curriculum. This is in order to understand the educational choices that students need to make in knowing what to learn. We look at curriculum development and theory, and consider the opportunities and restraints existing within the curriculum for students (and their tutors). We discuss what students and tutors need to know in order to make appropriate decisions that will ensure actions match learning needs. We then highlight the relationship between students' current and future needs and the tutor's role in helping to articulate and exemplify them. In this role the tutor needs to address choices in learning, individual purposes and targets, issues of negotiation and ownership. Reflection on these issues will highlight the importance of identifying the immediate and future purposes of any learning task and will help teachers, tutors and learners address the last of our three aspects of learning – knowing what to learn.

As we are most familiar with the circumstances in the UK, we use these to illustrate the issues relating to knowing what to learn. Curriculum dilemmas are, however, universal and the issues that we discuss here are, we think, identifiable within and transferable to most education systems and political arenas.

Curricular dilemmas

At the start of the twenty-first century, there is a discernible predisposition towards the argument for a distinctive curriculum in schools and colleges that offers knowledge and experiences which are different from those obtained through everyday occurrences (Moore and Young 2001). This is a move away from the content-free, child-centred, 'process is all' polemic of previous decades. Such shifts in emphasis are fundamental to formal education. The philosopher John Dewey (in Bredo 1999) saw them as a strength rather than a weakness. He believed that activity, educational or otherwise, is a transaction between people and environment co-evolving to form a joint history of development. Ideally, experience informs reason and *vice versa* to create intelligent social reconstruction.

The theories and practices that inform curricular debates are complex. They have driven a relentlessly changing curriculum, constantly seeking improved strategies for teaching and learning (Fullan 1991, 1993; Ainscow *et al.* 1995) and draw on the latest thinking from educational philosophers and researchers, and sometimes from practitioners. Inevitably, there has been one argument about what should be included in a worthwhile school curriculum (Lawton 1996; Kelly 1999; R. Moore 2000), and another about how a new learning agenda for the twenty-first century might look (Clarke 2000; Kress 2000; Moore and Young 2001). The age-old questions remain. For example:

- What are the purposes of the curriculum?
- What should be included in a curriculum?
- Who should have the power to determine the curriculum?
- Are the right learning outcomes or standards attained from the curriculum?

And these questions are joined by those of the current age:

- Is our curriculum appropriate for the twenty-first century?
- Are students making the appropriate curriculum choices?

What are the purposes of the curriculum?

What we are required to learn at school is, to a greater or lesser extent, influenced by the beliefs that policymakers hold about the purposes of the curriculum. The main rationale for a 'national' curriculum in the UK was reiterated in the Education Act of 1999 and was stated as:

- to establish an entitlement;
- to uphold standards;
- to promote continuity and coherence; and
- to promote public understanding (Department for Education and Skills 2001).

In most societies, there is consensus that the curriculum should be founded on a common body of knowledge that everyone needs to have mastered in order to function effectively in that society. In recent times, however, demands on this body of 'sacrosanct' knowledge have arisen from a variety of sources. As Tomlinson and Little (2000) point out, the explosion of knowledge, a more pluralist society, a clearer understanding of theories of learning and a change in the social milieu of many students have taxed those with an investment in the curriculum. How can all that is important be adequately covered when what is important for one group of students may be less so for another.

Similarly, the impact of globalization, with national governments competing for manufacturing and creative contracts, and striving for the ultimate prize of a high-skills, high-wage, knowledge-rich economy (Brown *et al.* 2001) has influenced the curriculum debate. To achieve such an economy, it is argued, citizens need more than substantive knowledge: they need to achieve flexibility, to see themselves as lifelong learners and be able to apply their ongoing knowledge in new and creative ways. Although the links between learning at school and economic performativity are hotly contested by academics such as Elliott (2000), the preference for a curriculum that encourages well-balanced, creative and independent learners is rarely denied.

Within a general stance that the curriculum should address appropriate experiences for all students, there are those who argue for the primacy of theoretical knowledge, measured by examination, and for distinguishing the elite. The belief here is that imparting academic knowledge is the major purpose of schools and colleges. It is this that distinguishes them from other organizations such as hospitals and businesses. In addition, one of the major functions of all levels of education is preparation and selection for the next stage. As individuals, this tends to be the view of the majority of students (and frequently their parents). Whether or not students see themselves as 'good' learners is dependent mainly on their grades compared with their fellow classmates, and, to some extent, on verbal and written feedback from subject teachers and tutors.

Others believe that utilitarian practical skills, leading directly or indirectly to employment, valued in the workplace and achievable by most, should be the focus of the required learning experience. Policymakers (see Callaghan 1976; Raffo 2003) have long suggested an association between the motivation for learning and clear perceptions that the content of learning is useful and applicable. Much of the current discourse about school improvement focuses on the development of measurable and marketable skills. Indeed, our research has shown (Bishop *et al.* 1999) that some subjects in the curriculum are deemed by students to be more important than others and hence are thought worthy of more concentrated study.

On the other hand, attempts to raise motivation by offering a more obviously relevant curriculum (examples in the UK include the Mini-enterprise in Schools Project, the Technical and Vocational Education Initiative and the School Curriculum Industry Project – see Roberts and Miller 1991) have had only limited success. While there is an obvious requirement for policymakers to ensure that the quality of the curriculum is unquestionable and matches the needs of contemporary society, our research suggests that the premise concerning pupil motivation was not well founded. Pupils, at heart, want to do well and are prepared to work hard to do so, but for some there is a barrier between their espoused desires and their practical achievement which seems to have little to do with curriculum content. An understanding of the purposes of the curriculum alongside the content of the curriculum could be a greater motivator for students.

Some educationists consider that the needs and preferences of the learner should be the central concern for curriculum developers. Prior to the establishment of the National Curriculum in 1988, a debate influencing the content and structure of the school experience had developed around the primacy of process or product. This recognized that subject knowledge, however presented, does not happen in isolation – the whole experience of the learning situation has an impact on what is learned. During the 1970s and 1980s, the belief that an understanding of the skills of learning was more important than any facts or substantive knowledge that might be learned came to the fore (Plowden 1967; Brandes and Ginnis 1986). Teachers and trainee teachers were urged to consider the substance, and to change

their delivery of the curriculum, to achieve more fully the goals of transferring the source of learning from the teacher to the students themselves.

Furthermore, regardless of the positions taken above (i.e. a curriculum
for the delivery of a discrete body of knowledge, a curriculum for the development of the workforce or a curriculum for personal development), there is
a fourth stance which may be something of a compromise. It is the model
that we are moving towards with post-14 students in the UK – a meld of
academic, cross-disciplinary and vocational knowledge.

But is there not a further purpose to the curriculum? There is an
explicit intention in the school curriculum in many countries (Kaplan
1997; Department for Education and Skills 2000) to mould citizens who will
contribute positively to their communities. For example, the following is
the mission statement of the Russian Federation, created after the break-up
of the USSR.

> **Towards an education of one's choice in the Russian Federation**
> *Today the strategy in the field of education is to facilitate the solution of
> global social problems through educational means,* in particular:
> * To strengthen and develop democracy;
> * To consolidate national identity, harmonize ethnic relations,
>   to ease social tensions;
> * To develop the national economy's potential under new con-
>   ditions
>
> *The way to accomplish these aims is through:*
> * Ensuring guarantees of citizens' rights to get an education;
> * Transition to an education of one's choice and ensuring an
>   opportunity to get education in accordance with one's talents,
>   abilities, interests and health;
> * Maintaining a common educational space;
> * Modification of the education content and its humanization;
> * Ensuring a high-quality education
>
> *The main direction of the reform* is to create certain conditions for a
> transition from a unified, standardized, uniform education *to an
> education of one's choice.* The educational system should change to
> meet educational needs of children, families and different com-
> munities.
>
> (Russian Federation 1996: 5)

In the UK, citizenship education is now a compulsory part of the curriculum in both primary and secondary schools. The aim of citizenship is
to provide students with the knowledge, skills and understanding that will

enable them to play an effective role in society. Citizenship education has three strands:

- *social and moral responsibility*: pupils learn, from the beginning, self-confidence and socially and morally responsible behaviour, both in and beyond the classroom, towards those in authority and each other;
- *community involvement*: pupils learn how to become helpfully involved in the life and concerns of their neighbourhood and communities, including learning through community involvement and service;
- *political literacy*: pupils learn about the institutions, issues, problems and practices of our democracy and how citizens can make themselves effective in public life, locally, regionally and nationally, through skills as well as knowledge (Department for Education and Skills 2000).

A curriculum for the twenty-first century

Whatever the degree of centralized control of the curriculum, schools and colleges also strive to identify and disseminate their own particular philosophy of education. This is often set out as a public statement in a prospectus or on a website, and intended to attract customers. In both the state maintained and the independent sectors, there is always tension between, for example:

- the ideals of individual support and development and the realities of group organization and timetabling;
- promoting improved levels of attainment in core areas such as literacy and numeracy against a broad and balanced curriculum; and
- the provision of vocational studies alongside the academic route.

Some institutions try to provide a broad experience. For example, those who offer a curriculum based on the International Baccalaureate (IB) subscribe to the mission statement set out by that organization as follows:

Through comprehensive and balanced curricula coupled with challenging assessment, the International Baccalaureate Organization aims to assist schools in their endeavours to develop the individual talents of young people and teach them to relate the experience of the classroom to the realities of the world outside. Beyond intellectual rigour and high academic standards, strong emphasis is placed on the ideals of international understanding and responsible citizenship, to the end that IB students may become critical and compassionate thinkers, lifelong learners and informed participants in local and world affairs, conscious of the shared humanity that binds all people together while respecting the variety of cultures and attitudes that makes for the richness of life.

(International Baccalaureate Organization 2002: 5)

There is a persistent conviction, however, that school activities designed around the transmission of subject knowledge are less helpful, in the long term, than those that are based on an understanding of important life themes. Observers such as Kress (2000) believe that the curricula of schools in western societies remain entrenched in the requirements of the nineteenth century while Clarke (2000) argued for the interconnected curriculum in the quotation at the beginning of this chapter.

The argument for the interconnected curriculum suggests that in the twenty-first century the basics of schooling, although crucial in providing a foundation for future development, are not sufficient either for the long-term needs of the labour market or the effectiveness of individuals as active members of society. This logic goes on to claim that knowledge of facts is not enough to ensure personal well-being (Hargreaves 2001; SCRE 2001). The explosion of knowledge since the mid-twentieth century means that individuals simply cannot retain in their own brains sufficient information for their needs. The development of knowledge in the next 50 years will mean that current facts and practice will soon be out of date (Killeen 1996). People need to be continually learning and relearning. They need to feel confident as learners and be aware of their thinking skills and processes.

Students should understand the purposes of the curriculum

In determining the most urgent and appropriate purposes of the curriculum it is not usual to consult the student. In the general scheme of things, what the young learner wants from formal education is not thought to be of great consequence. In truth, it is likely that most students have failed to contemplate the notion that there might be different outcomes for particular curricular models. Our research (Bishop et al. 1999; Bullock and Wikeley 1999) indicates that students tend to accept the current bodies of knowledge and systems as the norm and see them as hoops to jump through in their passage through education. For example, although most tutors saw the PLP project as an innovative pupil-led process, many students saw it as an established school process with the tutors asking questions and setting the agenda. In response to a question about the purpose of the one-to-one session, one student commented:

Male: Yes, we've had one-to-one with our tutors in Year 10 and 11 and now in Year 11 we've been saying, 'How would you go on to fill in your application form?' What you need to put down.

(Year 11 student, comprehensive school)

In short, the activities become the routines of school, and perhaps more worryingly, the routines of learning. The distinction here is that while we see the ultimate purpose of education as promoting creative thinkers and independent learners, the reality of schools and colleges is the organization of large and varied communities. In order to function effectively for all its community members, any school or college needs to establish rules of behaviour and routines of institutional life. One of the tasks of the tutors must be to work with their students to disentangle the routines of school from the processes of learning. In doing this, it can be beneficial for personal tutors to encourage students to articulate their individual expectations of what they will learn at school or college, and to compare these with the new and traditional purposes of the curriculum.

Which curriculum?

What students need to know at school and beyond is sometimes decided by personal choice, but more often seems to be a matter of happenstance. Whatever the curriculum offered, choosing the appropriate facts, theories and skills is in itself a fundamental life skill.

The main curriculum is usually considered to be the body of knowledge, skills and experiences that is set out as appropriate for students to learn and teachers to teach. Some countries such as the UK have legislated for centrally prescribed areas of study and levels of attainment appropriate for stages throughout compulsory education; while others such as the USA prefer a more flexible approach. There are many arguments (e.g. Lawton 1996; Marsh 1997; Kelly 1999) concerning what should be included in a curriculum. For example, different factions may argue for greater or lesser emphasis on:

* a body of fundamental knowledge that all people need to have to be fully functioning members of society;
* opportunities that contribute to vocational training and eventually improve the standard of the workforce;

- an inculcation of attitudes and values that contribute to an improvement in society;
- student-centred development to ensure that each individual reaches his or her potential;
- activities to promote thinking and creativity; and
- areas of aesthetic benefit.

Before 1988, in the UK the law had no authority over what was taught in schools – the school curriculum. Apart from the compulsory inclusion of religious education and the constraints of the public examination system, schemes of work in the various classrooms and subject areas were largely decided by headteachers, school governors and heads of department. While this gave enhanced professional status to teachers, there were many academics (see Lawton 1973), politicians and sectors of the business community (see Kelly 1999) opposed to this autonomy. These constituencies felt that a more prescribed curriculum offered advantages of entitlement, equal opportunities, accountability and, above all, improved standards, economy and efficiency.

These arguments were mirrored in other countries. In the UK they won the day; but they did not, by contrast, in Australia, where there are nationally agreed key learning areas but frameworks for curricula are determined within each state or territory. This system, it is argued, allows schools to adapt to local needs (Education Queensland 2001). The US government, on the other hand, does not determine what students should know and be able to do in any subject at any level of schooling. Expectations and standards for students' performance are the responsibility of state and local authorities and therefore vary greatly by state, district and even school (McCarty 2001).

In the UK, the statutory curriculum was established by the Education Reform Act of 1988. This National Curriculum set out the subject areas and programmes of study for 5- to 16-year-old students in state-maintained schools. The Act stated that the curriculum should be broad and balanced, and should promote the spiritual, moral, cultural and physical development of students. It also imposed new ways of judging and celebrating success in learning. The main components of the new curriculum were:

- three core subjects (English, mathematics and science);
- seven foundation subjects (modern languages, technology, history, geography, art, music and physical education);
- attainment targets for students at different levels;
- programmes of study for each subject; and
- assessment at four key stages.

The reality of the National Curriculum turned out to be a complex, overloaded and bureaucratic model and schools struggled with it until 1994, when the government set up a review of the National Curriculum. As a result of this consultation with teachers, a more pragmatic, less structured curriculum has been created for some students (Dearing 1994). Schools may now offer a work-related learning programme that gives 14- to 16-year-old students experience of the working environment and working practices, and also provides them with the opportunity to develop literacy, numeracy and other key skills through these focused activities. This experience can replace up to two subjects out of the following three: design and technology, modern foreign languages and science (Department for Education and Skills 2001).

Recent trends have not altogether been towards more flexibility, however. Classroom teachers who were accustomed to using their professional judgement to determine the ways in which topics were taught have seen some of that autonomy eroded by the introduction of the National Literacy and Numeracy Strategies (Earl *et al.* 2003). These strategies were introduced to primary schools in 1999 and 2000 respectively and to the early years of secondary schools (Key Stage 3) in 2001 as initiatives to raise standards. They aimed to improve classroom practice and pupil learning in literacy and mathematics by providing detailed teaching programmes and good-quality teaching materials.

Although the primary and early secondary school curriculum has inexorably become more rigid, this complexity of change has led, at the 14- to 19-year-old stage, to a proliferation of routes and possibilities sufficient to perplex the most focused and confident of students. In the UK at the beginning of the twenty-first century, academic, vocationally-related and occupational routes with differently moderated levels of attainment are available for selection by students aged 14 years and older (Dearing 1996; Department for Education and Skills 2001).

It is therefore crucial for students to be aware of the opportunities available to them through the curriculum, and to be able to make sensible and informed choices about how and what they study. In many schools and colleges, this task has already been delegated to tutors of classes approaching decision points. The implications of this responsibility may not be fully considered. As Hodkinson and Sparkes (1993) observed, new areas of expertise may have to be assumed by such tutors, so that access to the right facts and most appropriate options is available. In our discussions with teachers and students it was clear that what mattered to both was not only a good grade at the end of the course, but also the correct choice of courses as a first step on a future career ladder:

'The promise of success in the future is an incentive for students'
(PLP coordinator, comprehensive school).

The requirement for informed and expert practitioners to be appointed as tutors needs to be balanced by student preferences for approachable and available personal tutors with whom they feel comfortable (Bullock and Wikeley 1999; Bullock and Fertig 2003):

'With the personal tutor you can just go and have a chat if you want about just anything'
          (vocational qualification student, further education college).

The formal curriculum is not solely concerned with factual knowledge, and what pupils learn in schools is not, of course, confined to subjects set out in the National Curriculum. Students may need to be reminded of the other aims and outcomes from the curriculum and these may need to be more central within student-tutor discussions and planning. Also included in most curricula are issues of morality and behaviour. These are virtues very important to parents, employers and society (but are neither readily measured nor conveniently used as personal, institutional or national targets). Additionally, extracurricular activities are outside the legislated body of knowledge but they contribute to the overall aims and objectives of the institution. Extracurricular activities are offered in most schools and colleges and aim to offer opportunities to develop individual talents and interests. They include team games, musical groups, crafts and community projects.

Researchers such as R. Moore (2000) and Marsh (1997) have noted that alongside this authorized programme, the 'hidden curriculum' plays a significant part in students' development. The hidden curriculum has been identified as the learning that students gain from their place within the school or college community, but which is apart from the official syllabus. It may come from informal interactions with peer groups, individual teachers or from the osmosis of the prevailing culture and ethos of the school community, sending messages about values and beliefs to its students. It is often omitted from considerations of what and how students are learning:

'The hidden curriculum exercises a profound influence on students and continues to be overlooked by most teachers, which is unfortunate since the hidden curriculum can be a vehicle for delivering desirable ends'
          (Hargreaves 2001: 494).

Recently, transdisciplinary skills such as key skills and thinking skills have become more explicit within prescribed curricula. In England, from September 2002, a national framework for the teaching of personal, social and health education has included guidance to help all students develop an understanding of their own learning and performance. Students seeking a transdisciplinary qualification post-16 have been able, since September 2000, to take the Key Skills Qualifications. These are designed for use in a wide range of settings – schools, colleges, training, higher education and employment. They comprise:

- communication;
- application of number;
- information technology;
- working with others;
- improving own learning and performance; and
- problem solving.

The Welsh Baccalaureate, launched in 18 pilot schools and colleges in Wales in September 2003, has also included certification for key skills as part of its core assessed programme, while the shared features of the three developmental stages in the International Baccalaureate embrace a focus on developing skills for learning. These elements all acknowledge that education must also be about provision for students to develop the knowledge, skills and understanding they need to live confident, healthy, independent lives, as individuals, parents, workers and members of society (Department for Education and Skills 2000). Assessment for key skills in these curricula is, mainly, by portfolio and online or pencil and paper set tests.

While the arguments for a future scenario that rewards personal understanding and transdisciplinary skills are strong, the realities for students have changed little in recent decades. Students at transition points still need to make the best informed choices that their limited experiences will allow. Between the ages of 14 and 19 students have no conception of the knowledge or skills that they will need in the future. The next year or few years are the limits of their future planning:

> I don't think it's too early to start thinking about the future, but you shouldn't really have your whole life planned out.
> (Year 7 student, comprehensive school)

> There are quite a few people who have quite a few doubts about themselves personally. So it's hard for them, but I think the majority believe they could go to university later on.
> (Year 11 student, comprehensive school)

In an era where examination grades are regarded as critical by government, teachers and parents alike, students cannot be expected to value that which does not hold currency for the next few years of their lives. Key skills, when taught as a discrete subject, can be dismissed and disparaged as low level. When taught across the curriculum areas they are rarely identified or explicitly transferred to other subjects. Part of the role of the personal tutor must be to work in a cross-curricular capacity to provide opportunities for students to recognize and gather evidence of key skills, whether or not this leads to a recognized qualification.

Who determines the curriculum?

Having considered the purpose and content of the curriculum, a further question needs to be asked. Where does the authority lie to determine this body of knowledge that will empower learners (Schostak 2000)? The arguments of the 1970s and 1980s saw, on the one hand, the freedom of teachers to decide what was taught in schools, and how it was taught, as being the privilege of a liberal and democratic country (Barber 1996). On the other hand, policymakers agreed that as the school curriculum is the foundation of the future society, culture and workforce, it was too important to be left solely in the control of teachers (Lawton 1996). Curricula in educational institutions are now determined by an array of individuals and groups with diverse agendas. Typically, degrees of influence lie with sources such as:

- the government;
- government agencies;
- teacher unions and professional associations;
- examining bodies (such as the International Baccalaureate Organization);
- the media;
- academics;
- employers (adapted from Marsh 1997: 174).

In our arguments, we would not wish to suggest that it is undesirable for a curriculum to be designed by those who have accumulated wisdom of pupil development and who have practical experience of wide and generic learning needs. A programme needs to be planned to ensure that a rational and appropriate selection of content and experiences is available for all learners (Lawton 1996). Indeed, since the time of Plato and Aristotle, the curriculum has been shaped by social philosophers and political persuaders as well as by educational theorists. Further influences on the curriculum have, throughout the ages, come from religious groups, employers and the community. Needless to say, each particular group has tended towards a specific and distinct view of an ideal curriculum (R. Moore 2000). Factions have disagreed on the purpose of the curriculum, what the most advantageous outcomes from it should be and how skills and knowledge should be delivered in order to shape and socialize the citizens of the future. The struggle for primacy over curriculum matters has been, and will continue to be, intense:

> 'The reason why the curriculum can cause these eruptions of public controversy is that what we know affects who we are (or are perceived to be). Issues of knowledge entail issues of identity'
> (R. Moore 2000: 17).

The defining of the content of any curriculum is only the beginning. As important are matters of planning, pedagogy and organization. How the content is presented and delivered engages, or not, the student body. This is the responsibility of the teachers and it is their obligation (and power) to decide the experiences and activities that will enable the students to construct their learning. The teacher also determines the learning milieu of the classroom, the background material, the ethos and expectations, and the habitual procedures. The concern of the class or subject teacher is likely to be a group of around 30 disparate individuals. Inevitably, he or she must do what is best for the whole group.

Personal tutors have similar power over the conduct of one-to-one discussions – the milieu of the tutorial. Here the focus is on the sharing of ideas between an individual student and the tutor, and this educational relationship is different from the educational relationship between the teacher and whole class. The skills of the teacher are not necessarily those of the tutor, although all teachers may, more and more, be required to take the tutoring role. As tutors, we need to focus on the needs of the individual learner, who may only have a few valued minutes of our time. Hence, the milieu changes. Listening replaces talking; shared understanding replaces didactic delivery; accurate and positive feedback replaces assessment; and specific and attainable target setting replaces vague expectations.

However, students themselves must accept responsibility and make a positive choice to learn. Unfortunately, many students, particularly those in the compulsory stages of education, still see the major responsibility for their learning as lying with the teacher. In their research into pupils' and teachers' perceptions of good teaching and learning, Morgan and Morris (1999) point out that almost 60 per cent of pupils thought that 'learning more' in some subjects rather than others was something to do with the teacher, while only 23.3 per cent believed it was something to do with themselves. The common experience of the class group may have a bearing on this denial of responsibility. In contrast, one-to-one tutorials provide the opportunity for clear delineation of responsibilities. Here, shared discussions should lead to the identification and planning of the actions that the students themselves must take in order to achieve their personal learning goals.

The curriculum, assessment and standards

An important tenet of the National Curriculum is that it should be able to be assessed, so that the learning that has occurred can be plainly determined and demonstrated for all to see. The logic that is employed for this emphasis derives predominately from the purpose of assessment as a summative tool, providing an overall measure of performance. In many societies, test results are required as a means of discrimination between individual students who wish to transfer and progress within the education system or to a chosen career. For students (and their teachers), national examinations are 'high stakes' events. Many have noted (Main 1980; Black and Wiliam 1998; Bishop *et al.* 1999) that the great majority of students are highly motivated by the desire to obtain good grades in external examinations, although a significant minority are demotivated by assessment procedures (Gipps 1994). However, many students see learning for summative assessment as a discrete task for completion, ultimately judged by others with superior knowledge, and allocated appropriate marks or grades. Students believe that they have learned something if they can reproduce it for a required response at a specific time. They also perceive that this type of superficial learning (Riding and Read 1996) is the major route to success and hence motivation is increased. This belief is often strengthened by the culture and organization of the school:

> 'Grades are the ultimate criterion of one's success at school and if one's grades are not good, love of one's work is unlikely to be viewed as much of a compensation'
>
> (Sternberg and Lubart 1992: 249).

A further issue for summative assessment is the national concern about general levels of education. There is a perception that standards in UK schools and colleges are lamentably low compared with our European and international competitors and that this is detrimental to the economic health of the country (Department for Education and Skills 2001). This perception is coupled with a belief that a centralized system for the measurement of outcomes will serve to compare the performance of institutions and individuals, and hence push up levels of achievement. Counter to this stance, there are many (e.g. Brown *et al.* 2001) who argue that a narrow, prescriptive curriculum and assessment system is antithetical to a burgeoning, healthy, high-skills economy. They argue that although the link between standards of education and the economy has been claimed for many years, it has never been convincingly proved.

Many argue for summative assessment with the observation that education is financed by public money and controlled by institutions traditionally not transparent to public scrutiny. Educators have the power to affect the well-being and future of young people. Educational institutions need, therefore, to be accountable, and the publication of examination and test results is, perhaps, the most simple way of demonstrating standards. This relies on a view that it is possible to devise the appropriate instrument to measure quality. Simplicity, however, is not always the only, or the best, option for choice and the nature of the objective judgements that are possible from the scores is a matter of heated debate (see McPherson 1993; Broadfoot 2001; Hargreaves 2001).

While summative assessment clearly has its place, we argue here that well-focused, timely and constructive formative assessment is the greater aid to learning. Our research has left us in little doubt that in schools and colleges, assessment fuels the learning process (see Chapters 5 and 6). We do not, therefore, believe that assessment necessarily diminishes the processes or outcomes of learning, but that over-assessment serves purposes other than those connected with individual student learning. Effective assessment does not end in a mark or a grade. Opportunities for the implications of the grade to be discussed in one-to-one or small group situations and related clearly to students' future tasks and targets are vital. This process is likely to be the stimulus for motivating and encouraging learning and also the key to engendering an understanding of how to learn (see Gipps 1994).

A problem arises when teachers assume that students will perceive the demands of learning and assessment in the same way that they do. In fact, despite teachers' assertions that marking schemes have been shared with students, the students tend not to understand what the task or the assessment criteria actually require from them (Black and Wiliam 1998). Our observations have suggested that it is not sufficient to tell students in a whole-class situation. Illustrations, examples and models are required. Alternatively, in a one-to-one discussion with a personal tutor, positive, task-oriented feedback related to individual learning goals and discussion of evidence for quality can enhance meaningful learning.

Conclusions

In this chapter we have addressed the issues relating to the purposes of the curriculum, the content of the curriculum and who has the power to determine the curriculum. Intentionally, we have stressed the contested nature of knowing what to learn. Education is a value-laden activity and it is important that we, as personal tutors and teachers, have considered our own values in relation to those held by colleagues and others in the community. Tutors may wish to explore the dilemma that is encountered between the purpose of education to produce free thinking, creative individuals and the practicalities of schools that reinforce the established order. Tutors are unlikely to deny their personal values in their conversations with their students. It is important, therefore, that students know the debate underpinning curriculum ideals. Only then can they fully understand the choices available to them and ensure that their planned actions, both short and long term, are compatible with their values as well as with their learning needs.

8 Supporting students in knowing what to learn

Male 1:	*The curriculum tells you what to do, you tell yourself what to do because you want to be this or that.*
Male 2:	*It's like saying is this information pertinent to real life? Why do I have to learn this if it's not going to help me in future life?*
Researcher:	*And maybe thinking about your learning makes you realize that perhaps it isn't.*
Male 1:	*If we could be told why we're learning this. In real life how would this apply to us? At times in maths it has been explained to us how it would help.*
Male 2:	*You hear people around saying 'Four more weeks and then no German! No art!' and I think they enjoy that because you know where you're leading to. You know what's at the end.*

(Year 11 students, comprehensive school)

Introduction

On one level, knowing what to learn is a simple concept. It all depends on what you want to achieve and for students in formal educational institutions it can appear very simple. In the UK, concerns that educational standards are in decline have resulted in a prescribed curriculum with increasingly measured outcomes (Kelly 1999). The Education Reform Act of 1988 explicitly defined the subjects and programmes of study that were required to be covered by all children between the ages of 5 and 16 in maintained schools. In parallel, standard assessment tests (sometimes referred to as SATs), were introduced at four key stages throughout the compulsory curriculum. These tests at ages 7+ (Key Stage 1), 11+ (Key Stage 2), 14+ (Key Stage 3) and 16+

were thought to be essential for the monitoring and evaluation of pupils' performances, and hence educational standards. More recently, baseline testing on entry to formal schooling at age 5+ has been added to the battery of tests. The 'what to learn' is very clear – you learn what is needed to get a good set of recognized qualifications which will give you access to whatever it is you want, or need, to do next.

As we discussed in Chapter 7, the arguments supporting these legislative changes are, first, that in order to motivate the majority of learners, qualifications need to be practical and useful. The notion of learning as an end in itself is largely discounted as improbable and elitist (see Moore and Young 2001). Second, it is suggested that the key to the quality of learning in schools rests, for the most part, on sound quantitative measures of their procedures and outcomes (Fitz-gibbon 1993; McPherson 1993; Schagen 1995). The latter argument reasons that to be transparent and fair for all, clear and measurable criteria for success need to be identified. Achievement (or lack of achievement) can then be demonstrated unequivocally as a measure of learning. In addition, these measures can be used as benchmarks for future improvement and also for comparison and accountability of individuals and institutions. An opposing argument is that a prescribed curriculum defines and limits worthwhile knowledge while measured attainment is seen as the prime evidence of learning. The wider concept of learning as the product of taught interaction with meaningful knowledge, and individual students with diverse, but unique, skills and understandings to draw upon, is therefore sidelined (see also Fielding 1997; Lauder *et al.* 1998; Jamieson and Wikeley 2000).

However, for any one student in school or college this debate, or even the existence of a debate, is rarely made explicit. For students, and many teachers, the syllabus is set, and in order to do well in examinations students have to learn what their teachers tell them they need to know. And in this schools and colleges excel. Whether it is good Key Stage 1 results, or the GCSE grades needed to do A level courses, or the degree classification required for acceptance by elite law firms, teachers in schools, colleges and higher education institutions are experts in knowing what is needed to make the grade. This rather narrow view of learning still leaves some areas for negotiation, particularly in a system in which school subject choice defines which career route is taken. We address how this can be supported in the next section. However, we would also argue that there is a second aspect to knowing what to learn that is rarely addressed within schools and colleges. This is the contested nature of the curriculum. In the final section of this chapter we consider how schools and colleges might involve students in the debate about the evolving nature of the curriculum.

Choices for learning

Between subjects

In our lives, the choices we are required to make, whether limited or liberal, are inescapable and a crucial determinant of the kinds of lives we lead. As far as education is concerned, we can make choices about what we select to study and also about the ways in which we prefer to learn. School time and teacher time are limited. Students' time is also limited. In the UK, significant choices about subjects to study (or not) can be made from around 14 years of age and, at least in the short term, are often irrevocable. Many students make their choices from narrow and uninformed perspectives. Beliefs about the usefulness, value and worth of possible paths through the curriculum are often conveyed by hearsay and opinion. Burden and Nichols (2000) point out that students very quickly grasp the messages of the curriculum that are hidden in assessment arrangements and school systems. Most students, who are faced with choices around the age of 14, see the purpose of learning as being closely linked with future job opportunities (Wikeley and Stables 1999). One quote from a 14-year-old girl responding to the question, 'What is the purpose of learning?' is typical: 'To help you get a good job, to get good marks that will get you into a good university' (Year 9 student, independent school).

Watts (1993), among others, points out that choices need to be based on much more than the identification of a suitable employment area. An understanding of personal strengths, weaknesses and motivations, and the ability to weigh and prioritize alternatives are important factors in giving confidence that the most appropriate path has been selected. Preferred strategies for making informed choices need to be considered.

If 14-year-old students are to be given the responsibility to make fundamental decisions about their futures, support and guidance are needed. Some guidance will be available from home, but inevitably feedback from the school will have a major influence. Teachers and tutors have a responsibility to help students link their skills, knowledge and attitudes to the most appropriate opportunities in the complex range of academic and vocational choices. Subject teachers can give subject-specific comment, but the personal tutor can provide an opportunity for a more general discussion. The way in which choices are made at this early stage may well provide a template for future decision making. At all stages in their lives, individuals need to be able to make sensible, informed choices that will lead to learning and doing the right things. For example, discussions between tutor and student might include the following:

- clarification of the student's long- and short-term aims and priorities;
- identification of the various options;

- benefits and drawbacks of each option;
- fallback strategy if the preferred option does not work;
- what are the general strategies for making informed decisions?

From the age of 11, students study different subject areas in separate lessons. As we have discussed earlier in this book, it is often left to students themselves to make any connection between what is learned in one subject area and what is learned in another. Although this can be confusing to some students, the separation of subject areas is something that primary-school children look forward to when they anticipate their move to secondary school (Muschamp and Bullock 2003). However, when they reach Year 9 and have to choose which subjects to continue for external examination and which to drop, there is a need for them to reflect on their more long-term plans. The PLP initiative was founded on students making better, more informed choices in Year 9 at 13 years of age, when choosing their options for GCSE. It was sponsored by the Careers Service who took a broader view of careers education than matching school leavers to jobs. Students were expected to write action plans that related not only to their current situation but also to their long-term life plans. Option choices could then be made based on some informed life plan. At one level this is a very sensible approach, and for some students it enables a holistic view of learning that often appears at odds with the segmented approach to education that is the norm in mainstream schools and colleges.

The PLP tutors clearly saw a major role for themselves in helping students to focus on what they needed to do to improve their academic outcomes. Where they made connections with the students' lives outside school, it was often on the basis of asking them what they wanted to do next and what qualifications they would need to make it possible. Perhaps unsurprisingly, the students tended to interpret the process as putting the emphasis on achievement rather than learning, and saw it as very careers-oriented. Students often associated the one-to-one discussion with things like a trip to a 'World of Work' convention or the school's need for information on which to plan work experience placements. Many students felt that teachers did not know them well enough to comment on their future goals: 'We sort of said what we would like to do after we left school and I said to be an accountant or something like that and then when we spoke to Mrs X She basically told me to do a business management degree which wasn't what I really wanted to do' (Year 11 female, comprehensive school).

It is interesting to note, however, that the tutors themselves did not consider substantive knowledge of pathways to further and (or) higher education, qualifications and careers as prerequisites for tutors. It could be of course, as we have mentioned before, that because this is such an integral part of what schools and colleges see as their core business, it is so internalized that tutors do not consider it worth mentioning. But although PLP tutors themselves saw the tutorial provision as a way of improving learning, they also did not mention an understanding of learning skills and strategies as being necessary for a personal tutor. The centrality of such expertise in the role of the tutor needs to be strongly emphasized by schools and colleges in professional development sessions.

The students were clear that the process was about making choices, but that in itself can be problematic:

Researcher: PLP: why 'learning' plan?

Male 2: Because it's your own and refers to some things out of school.

Female: You are talking about what you want to do when you leave school.

Male 3: It's not all about learning. Quite a lot is about setting targets.

Male 1: It's not just educational. Personal and social skills more.

Researcher: Is that still learning?

Male 1: Yes, you are always learning.

Researcher: Do you think a process of thinking about your learning will help you to do better?

Male 1: Yes, because then you have direction and you know exactly what you want to do.

Female: Not really.

(Year 11 students, comprehensive school)

Within this group there is an example of two students who clearly have very different views. For one (male), knowing his future direction is clearly helpful, but for the other (female) there is a danger that in trying to make the curriculum more relevant, by linking it to the long-term targets of career choice, it actually becomes less relevant:

Student 1: You can't monitor them [long term targets], they can't monitor them and the whole thing becomes meaningless. They set targets but nobody is doing anything about it.

Student 2: [It's] hard to discuss your future when it's so far away.

(Year 11 students, comprehensive school)

For many students in mainstream schools some targets still appear very long term and vague. Some had a concern that they were being pressurized by tutors to make decisions that they did not want to make at this stage of their lives. Although the students would like tutors to make more connection between the actual curriculum and the world beyond school, not all agreed that setting targets and reflecting on their learning would actually help them achieve that goal any better: 'May help later in life but I'm not yet sure how' (Year 9 student, comprehensive school).

Teenagers live very much in the here and now and motivation is rarely increased by offering them 'jam tomorrow'. Some tutors commented that if there is too much focus on long-term plans then when those plans change motivation for learning is lost: 'there were one or two that got jobs rather than looking at college courses and they mentally dropped out of it. It was no longer important to them if they weren't going on' (PLP tutor, comprehensive school). And this was borne out by the student interviews:

> At the time I did my first PLP interview I was interested in becoming a computer programmer, so I had this teach yourself computer programming book which I set a target to complete and later I actually had a rethink and I thought I was having a lot of difficulty on that and I found a career of a lawyer far more interesting, so I've given up on that target and now I'm putting my effort into hoping to become a lawyer, barrister.
>
> (Year 11 female, comprehensive school)

Changing subject areas halfway through a two-year programme is rarely possible (or sensible), so choosing what to learn based on long-term aspirations that can (and will) change can be self-defeating.

Focusing on shorter-term targets, related to educational achievement, is much more likely to have an effect. But these are unlikely to be useful goals and indicators if they are set by some unknown, external source. To be worthwhile, targets need to be created and owned by the learner with individual development as the prime purpose. Feeling that you have some control over what you want to learn is a powerful motivator. One middle manager's view of the personal tutor's role included the following observation: 'I think the focus [of the personal tutorial] should be on learning, improving learning, and looking at the students' overall progress and attendance, setting targets or attitudes to study, motivation to study and so on. I think the other stuff is important but the key focus has to be that' (head of department, further education college).

However, some students (like the male student above) did appreciate the opportunity to write down their goals and ambitions and to think about how they might achieve them. They saw this as an opportunity to learn about themselves: 'It organizes you a bit more, it highlights areas that you may not have realized before that you weren't quite as good at and it gives you a way to know how you are going to improve' (Year 9 male, comprehensive school).

They also discussed their choices with other adults. This particularly applied to girls and what schools describe as higher ability students: 'I talk to my mum and that. Probably since after I did that really [the one-to-one interview with tutor]. I started talking to her about options and GCSEs and things afterwards' (Year 11 female, comprehensive school).

The feedback from this research also enabled the careers guidance company to address these broader issues. The PLP initiative developed within the context of new thinking about careers education and the move away from careers choice to engagement with broader transferable skills.

Within subject choice

Choice can be more fundamental than subject options and future career areas. It can permeate and inform the processes of learning. It is clear from our research (Bullock *et al*. 2002) that independent learning requires decision making at all stages in a learning task (see also Wallace 2001). For example, students carrying out their own coursework projects were required to:

- reflect on the task and select a focus for the study;
- select information about the topic;
- think about, question and analyse the data;
- work with others;
- organize the data into findings or arguments;
- present the findings; and
- evaluate the product.

Although students used variations of these descriptors to explain their learning, it seemed that only a few had consciously reflected on the choices at these different stages. One student explained her choices as follows:

> You need to be critical of yourself and read it through and be able to see where you need to improve and you need to point out bits where you need to change it. It is about judging for yourself. I suppose in geography, before we went out to do all the work you need to think how appropriate it's going to be before you get there. Obviously it's not going to be appropriate to count traffic at every single outlet at one of the roundabouts. It just wouldn't be practical, so you have to think critically about what you're going to do before you attempt to do it.
>
> (Year 10 student, comprehensive school)

Nonetheless, when probed about their perceptions of learning, 16-year-old students indicated that the element of independent choice in coursework gave rise to challenge and effective learning. Both tutors and teachers have a crucial role to play in challenging pupils to provoke deeper thought processes. Challenging tactics that have been identified include supporting students to:

- decide how and where to get information;
- justify the choices they have made;
- decide how to organize and present their information most effectively; and
- reflect on and make judgements about the quality of the activity.

Sharing those choices

In colleges, where courses tend to be more focused and involve fewer subject areas, there is much discussion from both students and tutors about whether there are virtues in students having the same person as their subject teacher and personal tutor. Many students feel that there are positive aspects to this, in that it means that their tutor will be aware of the issues facing them within the classroom. In the best examples we came across, this enabled work in the tutorial session to be tightly focused around the specific learning needs of students. There was evidence here of sound target setting by personal tutors that was closely related to course requirements and specific learning objectives.

On the negative side, there was evidence that the alignment of subject teacher and personal tutor encouraged some tutors to see the tutorial as little more than an opportunity to deal with work that had not been covered during their subject sessions. With such tutors, this role merger appeared to detract from tutorial rather than from subject responsibilities, and a lack of awareness of the nature and purpose of tutorial provision in the institution was apparent (see also Green 2002). This clearly suggests that the 'profile' of tutorial expectations and provision needs to be unequivocal, particularly for staff with the dual role.

Once again however, thought has to be given to how, if students are setting their own targets, they can be put into operation. Where students were involved with more than one subject teacher, the mechanisms for communication between themselves, their personal tutor and the subject teachers were often unclear. This was a common organizational weakness that reduced the effectiveness of one-to-one discussions in particular cases. If the written plan is owned by the student, the responsibility for action should lie with him or her, and the procedures for requesting time with other teachers or adults should be clear. Otherwise, agreement about sharing plans and targets with others should be part of the dialogue and recorded in the written plan. For some, the awareness that the plan would be available to other teachers was a disincentive, as the following shows:

Female: A lot of them [the boys] thought they wouldn't write down anything that meant anything to them because other people were going to look at them.

Researcher: So there's a confidentiality issue.

Female: Yes.

Researcher: Do you feel that as well?

Female: Yes.

(Year 9 student, comprehensive school)

Although the confidentiality of the one-to-one discussion had rarely been considered, most students readily trusted their personal tutors with confidences both within and beyond academic aspirations. However, the nature of the relationship between the tutor and the student was more an issue for teachers rather than students. Positions that could be adopted within the role, and might potentially conflict with each other, were cited as: source of information; friend, mentor and guide; motivator and persuader; advocate; disciplinarian. All but the last have a role in helping students make choices, and even that can be useful in that students, in justifying their choices, may be helped to articulate the rationale in choosing them. But it appeared that the stance tutors favoured was strongly dependent on their personality and prior experiences as tutors. The majority of teachers and lecturers had formulated a clear rationale for the prime purposes of the tutor role, and had developed approaches and activities consistent with that. Others were troubled by the tension between different aspects of the relationship and, in consequence were less focused in their planning and approach. Although not necessarily less experienced as subject teachers, the latter group felt they would benefit from clarification of the role of the tutor and from sharing good practice in one-to-one activities and approaches.

The contested curriculum

And as we have reiterated throughout this book, learning is a highly personal activity. If 'interest' is such a key factor (Hidi 2003) in motivating learning, then supporting students in their understanding of knowing what to learn is important. But in this section we deviate from our other 'practical' chapters to discuss how to support an area of learning that we have not seen in any of the schools involved in the research supporting our ideas.

As we explored in the previous chapter, the curriculum is a highly contested concept. We would argue that students need to understand this and to become familiar with the debate about the validity of any particular curriculum, its position within a broader body of knowledge and the rationale underpinning why this particular part is presented. It may be the part that students need to be successful in the examinations set by a particular examining authority, but it is still only one small part. This is even more important as we move into the twenty-first century, when teachers are no longer the holders of knowledge, and global communication means that any one body of knowledge is increasing exponentially within very short time frames. Helping students understand the purposes and objectives of their learning enables them to see any one small part as a contributor to a much greater whole. This understanding has to be the basis of lifelong learning.

Young (2003) argues that there is a set of formal knowledge that students need help to access in order to become educated adults, and this is the role of the school and college curriculum. But we would argue that students also need to know that the content of this curriculum has been chosen from a wider body of knowledge, and what has been included has involved value judgements about what, or what is not, important knowledge. Understanding the politics of who chooses the content of the curriculum is vital if students are to understand how choices have been made, just as it is important to understand the cultural, ideological or national influences. Curricula such as literature and history can easily be seen to be nationally biased – very few students in English schools are ever taught Chinese history, for example. But other curricula areas are equally limited. Mary Jane Drummond (2001) writes about the contested nature of the early years curriculum by comparing: the Schools Curriculum and Assessment Authority (SCAA) publication entitled *Desirable Outcomes for Children's Learning on Entering Compulsory Education*, with its emphasis on the importance of early achievement in literacy; the Rudolf Steiner schools, with their provision of an environment focusing on the good and the beautiful in which children can have the best experiences rather than only those that reflect 'real' life; and the Reggio-Emilia approach in Italy that 'fosters children's intellectual development through a systematic focus on symbolic representation' (Edwards *et al.* 1994 in Drummond 2001: 91). These schools have resident artists who support 'the children's powers to represent their experiences, their questions, their problems and their dreams' through the provision of a wide variety of media. These three very different curricula all claim to provide the best grounding for children at the beginning of their formal education and their supporters would argue long and hard for their particular approach. If students are to become true lifelong learners and make well-informed decisions about what they need to know, then they must have an understanding of this debate.

The only example we have found where this debate is explicitly addressed with students is in those schools adopting the International Baccalaureate Diploma Programme. This programme includes a compulsory course entitled Theory of Knowledge (TOK) which has the specific aim of helping students become aware of the complex nature of knowledge by a 'thoughtful and purposeful enquiry into different ways of knowing and into different kinds of knowledge' (International Baccalaureate Organization 2003: 6). The curriculum for this course is based on a series of questions such as 'How do I know, how do we know, that a given assertion is true, or a given judgement is well grounded?' and covers three substantive topics: Knowers and Knowing; Ways of Knowing and Areas of Knowledge, which are linked by a series of questions that explore the connections between them. In our previous chapters, we expounded the notion that in order to help students know how to learn, tutors have to expose themselves as learners. The guidance notes for teachers of the TOK programme explicitly acknowledge that the concepts underlining the grouping of the questions into broad areas are of course in themselves contestable – i.e. the teachers must also enter the debate. The curriculum is thus intended to help students become aware of the interpretive nature of knowledge, including personal and ideological biases, and in doing so explore interdisciplinary connections.

The emphasis on developing an understanding of the critical examination of knowledge claims is supported through a set of linked questions. For example, when considering mathematical knowledge, it is suggested that teachers explore with students such questions as:

- Mathematics has been described as a form of knowledge which requires internal validity or coherence. Does this make it self-correcting? What would this mean?
- How is mathematical proof or demonstration different from, or similar to, justifications accepted in other areas of knowledge?
- Is mathematical knowledge certain knowledge?
- Could there ever be an 'end' to mathematics?
- Has technology – for example, powerful computers and electronics calculators – influenced the knowledge claims made in mathematics?
- Is the formation of mathematical knowledge independent of cultural influence? Is it independent of the influence of politics, religion or gender?

Questions for the natural sciences include:

- Is scientific method a product unique to western culture, or is it universal?
- What values and assumptions about knowledge underpin science?

An example in history is as follows:

- The study of the writings of history is not a study of all the past, but rather a study of those traces that have been deemed relevant and meaningful by historians. The availability of those traces, and their relevance and meaning, may be influenced in many ways by factors such as ideology, perspective or purpose.

While arts teachers might explore:

- Is originality essential in the arts? Is the relationship between the individual artist and transition similar in all cultures and times?
- In what ways does technology influence the arts? What, for example, might be lost or gained aesthetically by recycling visual images, or by composing music on a computer?

(IBO 2003:6)

It is not that these sorts of question are *never* addressed in other class-rooms – no doubt they are – but we have not seen anywhere else where the contestable nature of the whole curriculum is so explicit. Making connections between the content of one subject area and that of another could be an important undertaking for the personal tutor – asking questions that probe the reasons for learning might be equally valuable:

Researcher: Do you think the process of thinking about your learning would help you to do better at GCSE or wherever?

Male 1:   Yes, I think so, because then you know it's like a reason why you're learning something. You think about what you want to do.

Male 2:   If we could be told why we're learning this. In real life how would this apply to us? At times in maths it has been explained to us how it would help.

(Year 11 students, comprehensive school)

Conclusions

In this chapter we have raised the issues that schools and colleges need to address when trying to help students know what to learn. We have left this strand until last because in some ways it is the most obvious task for tutors – students need to learn what it is they need to know in order to pass their examinations – but in others it is the most difficult. Teachers of a single subject area are usually the holders of the knowledge needed to pass their particular examination, and personal tutors cannot know all subjects intimately enough to discuss the detail with students. If the tutor is to support the student in knowing what to know, then they need to be making connections across and beyond the classroom. However, as we have pointed out, trying to connect learning in school with the wider context of life is not always the most appropriate way of encouraging student learning. We therefore argue that involving students in the debate about broader aspects of the curriculum should enable them to make more informed choices about what to learn here and now. Helping them to develop a bigger picture of the curriculum and its constituent parts assists students to make meaning of their lives. They may think that in 'Four more weeks [there may be] no German! No art!', but what they have learned in those subject areas will enable them to engage with other areas later in their lives with a greater knowledge and understanding.

9　Educational relationships

... the quality of the relationships the teacher has with her class is not just desirable in itself but has an impact on the quality of the learning.

(MacGilchrist *et al.* 1997: 50)

Introduction

We have argued throughout this book that there are three strands to personal learning: knowing what to learn; knowing how to learn; and knowing oneself as a learner. These strands are tightly intertwined and if one is neglected the whole process of learning is diminished. Although we have tried to identify the main characteristics of each strand in the preceding chapters, many may have disagreed with our interpretations. We have no quarrel with this. The intention was never to write a recipe book. This is not a 'how to learn' manual and we are not providing right answers. Rather, we are identifying issues that can usefully be considered by all those involved in the processes of learning. In this book, we have focused on the practice of learning in secondary schools and colleges and have explored the role of the personal tutor in supporting this learning.

Our belief is that learning is personal for each individual. Learners are not machines or computers with predictable and measurable reactions to each input or stimulus. Hence, no one book can provide the right answers for each learner. Learners, themselves, change with experience or according to the task, and teaching approaches must differ from phase to phase of education, between subject areas and within social contexts. Teachers know that different groups of students will respond differently to the same lesson, while the same group can change their behaviour and reactions from day to day or even from lesson to lesson. Theories of learning and schemes of teaching, alone, do not account for the subjective nature of the school and college experience.

Our model of the practice of learning in schools and colleges derives essentially from sociocultural theories, in that we have a clear view of learning as a social process involving individuals or groups in activities where there is a 'more capable other' (Vygotsky 1978, 1986) who supports the learner(s) to a position of increased capability in terms of knowledge, skills or understanding. At every level, learning can be supported and extended by more capable others. More capable others include teachers, adults other than teachers, family and peers. We argue that, in a time of social and educational complexity, uncertainty and change there is an increasing role in schools and colleges for personal tutors who have the responsibility of discussing and supporting students' learning on an individual basis. We have suggested that the tutoring role can also be a learning experience for the tutor. Philip and Hendry (2000) observed that adult mentors working with young people interpreted mentoring as a form of 'cultural capital' for themselves. They identified four ways in which mentors benefited from their work with young people:

- it enabled them to make sense of their own past experiences;
- it was an opportunity to gain insights into the realities of other people's lives and to learn from these;
- it had potential to develop alternative kinds of relationships which were reciprocal and across generations;
- it built up a set of psycho-social skills as 'exceptional adults' able to offer support, challenge and a form of friendship (Philip and Hendry 2000: 218).

We describe the learning interactions between learners and a more capable other as an 'educational relationship'. An educational relationship can be formal or informal, implicit or explicit. In the main, the student–personal tutor educational relationship needs to be both formal *and* explicit. The emphasis must always be on the development of learning and it will continue only while the student belongs to an institutional or, perhaps, form or class group. Interpersonal interactions are invariably set within a milieu or context and the culture of the institution, therefore, has an impact on them. Each educational relationship will be unique but will, at the same time, be fashioned by the prevailing culture of the school or college.

Educational relationships and school culture

The culture of an institution is identified by the significant understandings, values, traditions and social practices that are accepted, often subconsciously, and shared by the individuals within it (Hofstede 1991; Angier and Povey 1999). In their work in mathematics classrooms, Angier and Povey point out that the culture of a classroom is: 'not fixed but shifting, contested and problematic: it will vary, perhaps considerably, over time, from day to day and even from moment to moment. Equally, each participant will experience that culture differently, reflecting each individual's identities and positioning' (1999: 147).

Thus, we perceive institutional culture as an accumulation of behaviours and beliefs that combine into an overarching 'way of doing things around here' that is shared by teachers and students. This is complex and dynamic, but students, as we argued in Chapter 7 in regard to curriculum content, also become accustomed to the institutional culture that is prevalent at their point in time. Dimmock and Walker (2000) maintain that culture is learned, not inherited, and one of the underlying purposes of educational institutions is to orientate students to a particular cultural perspective. The culture of what it means to learn and study that is encountered between the ages of 14 and 19 is likely to persist for many years, or until challenged by a different context.

In his seminal work with the multinational computer company IBM, the industrial psychologist Geert Hofstede (1991) identified four dimensions on which national cultures differ. These are 'power distance', 'uncertainty avoidance', 'individualism-collectivism' and 'masculinity-femininity'. Despite a concern whether or not market models and concepts from the business world should be imported into education, Dimmock and Walker (2000) have adapted and extended Hofstede's four dimensions to six in an educational context. They have used 'consideration-aggression' in place of 'masculinity-femininity' and added 'generative-replicative' as an indicator of predisposition to the generation of new ideas and methods; and also 'limited relationship-holistic relationship' as a gauge of the characteristics and importance of interpersonal relationships. Dimmock and Walker, however, caution that dimensions may be useful in clarifying a situation but are, nonetheless, constructed concepts and should not be reified. They also stress that dimensions of culture within a society may not be the same as those within an organization.

Despite such warnings, it is both illuminating and constructive to understand something of one's own culture. If an organizational culture is understood, it can be better managed to support the apposite ethos. Drawing on Hofstede and Dimmock and Walker, aspects of culture that could usefully be considered by schools and colleges include:

- *Power distance*. How is power exercised in the organization? Where do the students fit into the power distribution? Are teachers seen as the source of all knowledge or can the students' voice be heard (Praechter 2001)?
- *Attitude to change*. Does the institution believe they can embrace change positively in order to improve and move forward or does it prefer to work in a tried and tested way (Stoll and Fink 1996)?
- *Institutional expectations*. In the institution is there stress on competition and academic achievement or social harmony and wider success (Hargreaves 1999)?
- *Educational relationships*. What are the characteristics and importance of interpersonal relationships between tutors, teachers, students and parents? Within the institution are educational relationships systematic and formal or open and responsive (Fielding 2001)?
- *Common practices*. For example, is there a common language, or a process for creating a common language or vocabulary, through which educational ideas can be shared and individual progress can be facilitated and celebrated (A. Moore 2000)?

The need for the personal tutoring process to become embedded in school culture (Bullock and Wikeley 1999, 2003) also raises issues of communication and continuity. Schools and colleges understand that it is essential for the process to be consistent with the accepted values and traditions in the institution. In several schools that we visited, the personal learning planning coordinators identified a need to establish shared routines and recognized and systematic links between:

- school practice in successive years (in this case, these were Years 9, 10 and 11);
- student and/or tutor feedback to subject teachers, not necessarily involved in the PLP programme; and
- coherence and integration with other initiatives in the institution.

Some schools had already attempted to create structured ways of doing this. One strategy was to contextualize the PLP process and product within other research on learning (e.g. Joyce *et al.* 1997; MacGilchrist *et al.* 1997). This was felt to be a helpful way of introducing the initiative to other staff. The need to have a view of the 'big picture' if learning about learning is to be seen as relevant was acknowledged as important. Biggs and Moore's (1993) description of effective learning emphasizes the need for monitoring and regular review. As we have already stressed, tutors often feel that there is very little opportunity in schools and colleges for revisiting targets and reviewing progress. Consequently, learning is seen as a process of completing discrete and relatively undemanding tasks and not as an ongoing and challenging developmental journey. Similarly there is little opportunity in some schools and colleges for tutors, collectively, to relate to each other and to develop their own educational relationships. The need for tutors' learning processes to mirror those in which they are engaging their pupils was obvious in the schools in our research (Bullock and Wikeley 1999, 2003) where importance was attached to such discussions.

Educational relationships and communication

Educational relationships, like all relationships, are founded on communication. Good communication skills are essential in all educators. Requirements for good communication include immediacy, listening, observing, understanding, shared language and respect. It is possible to convey some of this without words, but for the most part conversational exchanges are required.

In a student-personal tutor conversation, there may be a gap between the perspectives of the student and those of the tutor. This may be in terms of the requirements for learning and also in terms of the capability of the tutee. There is also an inevitable gap in the power relationship. Normally, in a learning context, the more capable other has the greater power (Edwards 2001). In addition, there are clear superordinate and subordinate relationships in schools and colleges. Bearing in mind Wood's (1998) observation in a range of classroom situations that the more the teacher asks questions the less the students have to say, the personal tutor may need to consider how he or she can stimulate a fitting, but less controlling, interaction in the one-to-one setting: 'if other goals are also being sought – for example, encouraging children to reason out loud, to ask questions of their own, to state their own opinions, ideas and uncertainties, or to narrate – then the frequent use of specific, closed questions will not bring about the desired ends (Wood 1998: 174–5). Stimuli or probes that expect some deliberation and reflection on the part of the student are more likely to generate rich and insightful conversations, and ultimately greater student power and confidence.

We found some of the ideas of Eric Berne (1975), the developer of transactional analysis, useful here. Berne suggested that the human personality is made up of three 'ego states', each of which is a discrete composition of thought, feeling and behaviour, that we use when interacting with each other. The ego states are:

- *parent* (an authority figure that can be either nurturing and comforting or critical and judgemental);

- *adult* (a logical and objective thinker); and
- *child* (an emotional thinker that can be compliant and fearful or combative and angry).

Berne's argument was that ego states are neither good nor bad and each is used in particular situations. All three states have functional and dysfunctional aspects, but the quality and effectiveness of communication are improved if the more capable other can recognize the ego state of both participants in an educational relationship. Berne also observed that people need what he called 'strokes' – the units of interpersonal recognition to survive and thrive. Positive strokes reinforce self-esteem. Negative strokes do not do this, but even they can be better than being ignored. In any educational relationship strokes are both given and received. Understanding how you as a tutor or teacher give and receive positive and negative strokes and changing unhealthy patterns of stroking are powerful aspects of work in transactional analysis.

As we pointed out in Chapter 4, the dialogue needs to start with clarification. Assumptions, misinformation and lack of knowledge need to be identified and converted into an exchange that leads to a meaningful and shared understanding. Experiences and perceptions need to be articulated and labelled so that both parties find common ground and understand each other:

> In working with persons to discover learning needs, we are encouraging them to name certain of their experiences as needs – i.e. learning requirements which are fundamental to them – and then give names to those needs. More importantly, we are encouraging them to view their needs as belonging to them as individuals, decontextualized from the social relations that frame their life possibilities. We are helping persons to construct identities for them ... and this is not a neutral process.
>
> (Edwards 2001: 45)

Conversations are not always well remembered. In Chapters 4 and 6, we discussed the importance of capturing the learning plan or action plan. The general nature and tone of the discussion may be recalled, but the detail can often be lost in the volume of information exchange and the fog of competing thoughts. Some students (and tutors) may find it hard to concentrate and, at the end, be unable to bring to mind what has been heard, as opposed to what they themselves have said. Personal tutors need to recognize this imbalance and act accordingly. Active listening is paramount. Note-taking is a simple strategy, but may overly formalize the one-to-one meeting. We have heard of audio recording being used successfully with students, each having their own tape to act as an *aide mémoire* for the subsequent writing of the personal learning plan. A few minutes set aside at the end of the dialogue for student and tutor to reflect on the experience and to recall jointly the main points of the discussion also works well.

Educational relationships as motivators

We have entitled this book *Whose Learning?* for a reason. Parents, teachers and tutors readily make the assumption that learning is for the young person but, if asked, many students would suggest that much of their learning is in order to please others – parents, teachers, tutors and so on (Beltman 2003). In earlier chapters we discussed the social nature of learning as a process but not the social nature of learning as an outcome.

In school or college, a prime motive for learning is the attempt to earn status, esteem, approval and acceptance in the eyes of friends, peers, parents and teachers (see Hargreaves *et al.* 1982; Norwich 1999). These rewards may be short-term by means of good marks and teacher praise or long-term through entrance to careers and higher education. The avoidance of reprimands and punishment can also be a motive for learning. In some cases the reverse can be true when peer groups gain status through poor work and disruptive behaviour. This type of motivation has been called 'extrinsic motivation' (Gage and Berliner 1984; Willis 1990).

On the other hand, 'intrinsic motivation' implies curiosity or interest in the learning task for its own sake (Gage and Berliner 1984; Willis 1990). Research (Main 1980; Bishop *et al.* 1999) has demonstrated convincingly that the majority of students are motivated to learn by external factors such as examinations. Students perceive national examinations as an important standard and also as a selector for future options. They want to achieve good results. Students' comments indicate, however, that this is almost entirely extrinsic motivation and has little to do with interest in a particular subject area. As we illustrated in Chapter 7, Sternberg and Lubart (1992: 249) made a similar point when they suggested that love of one's work is unlikely to be viewed as much of a compensation for poor grades.

Those who are intrinsically motivated (and this appears to increase when students are given control of their own learning) are more likely to be autonomous, successful learners. For those who are motivated by extrinsic factors, learning can be more uncertain and more likely to be influenced by peer groups. One contention for effective learning from our research is that, at the critical stages in secondary school and further education the impetus for learning rests powerfully upon peer group dynamics as well as individual motivation. Teachers and learners constantly need to be aware of the social structures and cultures within the school which create their own motivational effects (Gage and Berliner 1984; Thrupp 1997). Friendship groups can be powerful sources and stimulators of learning. On the other hand, for students who have little hope of success in school terms, failure as a group is infinitely less threatening and can still provide the sense of belonging and personal security (Willis 1990).

Maslow (1970) arranged motivating factors in a hierarchy of needs to be satisfied with basic physiological needs such as food and water, followed by safety factors such as security and warmth as the fundamental necessities which must be fulfilled before the next level can be accessed. The need for esteem and respect in terms of status, achievement and competence within a group comes towards the top of the hierarchy, with only self-actualization or the realization of one's potential above them. As the majority of students in their middle teens are unlikely to be at the point of understanding the gratification derived from realizing their own potential, acceptance within the group is likely to be the most powerful motivating factor: 'People are automatically motivated to learn whatever they need to learn in order to become a member of the community to which they want to belong' (Abbott 1994: 46).

It is clear that the need to belong is a prime motivator. This can work counterproductively, however, and the whole-class setting may not always be appropriate. Removing individuals from the influence of a particular peer group, even for a short action planning dialogue or for a longer piece of coursework, may have far-reaching benefits. Concentrating on bolstering self-esteem and exploring strategies for learning in one-to-one discussions with students who rate themselves as less capable, might bring about an immediate increase in tutors' influences over lower achieving students. It is possible for such a conversation to be both challenging and non-threatening.

In the present debate about the lower achievement of boys, both finding and funding the time to listen to their experiences and concerns and to discuss their strategies for learning may be worth wider consideration. From our research, it would appear that the entitlement for all does marginally outweigh the focusing of limited funding on a specific, particularly needy group. However, any additional resources may be best used with such groups – for example low attaining boys.

Conclusions

In this book we have tried to unravel the complex process of supporting young people through their formal learning experiences in schools and colleges. We have deliberately highlighted the role of the personal tutor, partly because the role has become more common in recent years, but also because it allowed us to focus our thinking purely on what we call 'learning practice'. Focusing on the needs of the individual learner changes the milieu from that of the subject-focused classroom: listening replaces talking; shared understanding replaces didactic delivery; accurate and positive feedback replaces assessment; and specific and attainable target setting replaces vague expectations.

We have also identified three strands that we think are the important elements of 'learning practice'. These are:

- knowing what to learn;
- knowing how to learn; and
- knowing oneself as a learner.

Having unravelled the strands, we have, in this last chapter, re-ravelled them again. The world is a complex place and increasingly becoming more complex. In order to cope with that complexity, young people need to ravel and re-ravel their own yarn of learning. They need to understand their own approach to the personal activity of learning about, changing with or even adapting to lots of different experiences. We hope we are offering teachers and tutors something on which to reflect in order that they can give the students with whom they have an educational relationship the support that they need to become confident, knowledgeable adults.

References

Abbott, J. (1994) *Learning Makes Sense: Re-creating Education for a Changing Future*. Letchworth: *Education 2000*.

Ainscow, M., Hargreaves, D. and Hopkins, D. (1995) Mapping the process of change in schools: the development of six new research techniques, *Evaluation and Research in Education*, 9(2): 75–90.

Angier, C. and Povey, H. (1999) One teacher and a class of school students: their perceptions of the culture of their mathematics classroom and its construction, *Educational Review*, 51(2): 147–60.

Argyris, C. and Schön, D. (1974) *Theory in Practice: Increasing Professional Effectiveness*. San Francisco: Jossey-Bass.

Ausubel, D. and Robinson, F. (1969) *School Learning: An Introduction to Educational Psychology*. London: Holt, Rinehart & Winston.

Bailin, S., Case, R., Coombs, J.R. and Daniels, L.B. (1999) Common misconceptions of critical thinking, *Journal of Curriculum Studies*, 31(3): 269–83.

Barber, M. (1996) *The Learning Game: Arguments for an Education Revolution*. London: Indigo.

Beltman, S. (2003) *Fostering the will to learn: motivation is socially shaped*. Paper presented at the European Association for Research on Learning and Instruction 10th Biennial Conference, University of Padova, Italy.

Benson, P. (2001) *Teaching and Researching: Autonomy in Language Learning*. Harlow: Longman.

Berne, E. (1975) *Transactional Analysis in Psychotherapy*. London: Souvenir Press.

Bernstein, B. (1988) Education cannot compensate for society, in R. Dale, R. Fergusson and A. Robinson (eds) *Frameworks for Teaching*. London: Hodder & Stoughton.

Biggs, J.B. and Moore, P.J. (1993) *The Process of Learning*, 3rd edn. Englewood Cliffs, NJ: Prentice Hall.

Bishop, K.N., Bullock, K.M., Martin, S. and Thompson, J.J. (1999) User's perceptions of the GCSE, *Educational Research*, 41(1): 33–47.

Bishop, K.N., Bullock, K., Martin, S. and Reid, A. (2003) Learning from coursework: student voices, teacher choices, *Topic*, 30(6): 1–7.

Black, P. and Wiliam, D. (1998) *Inside the Black Box: Raising the Standards through Classroom Assessment*. London: Kings College School of Education.

Bloom, B.S. (1956) *Taxonomy of Educational Objectives: The Classification of Educational Goals*. London: Longman.

Bornholt, L.J. (2000) Social and personal aspects of self knowledge: a balance between individuality and belonging, *Learning and Instruction*, 10(5): 415–29.

Boud, D. (1995) *Enhancing Learning Through Self-assessment*. London: Kogan Page.

Boud, D. and Walker, D. (1998) Promoting reflection in professional courses: the challenge of context, *Studies in Higher Education*, 23(2): 191–206.

Boud, D., Keogh, R. and Walker, D. (eds) (1985) *Reflection Turning Experience into Learning*. London: Kogan Page.

Bourdieu, P. and Passeron, J.C. (1990) *Reproduction in Education, Society and Culture*. London: Sage.

Bowl, M. (2002) The learning society: researching the rhetoric, *British Educational Research Journal*, 28(4): 623–9.

Brandes, D. and Ginnis, P. (1986) *A Guide to Student Centred Learning*. Oxford: Blackwell.

Bredo, E. (1999) Reconstructing educational psychology, in P. Murphy (ed.) *Learners, Learning and Assessment*. Buckingham: Open University Press.

Broadfoot, P. (1997) Assessment and learning: power or partnership, in G. Stobart and C. Gipps (eds) *Assessment – A Teacher's Guide to the Issues*. London: Harper & Row.

Broadfoot, P. (2001) Empowerment or performativity? Assessment policy in the late twentieth century, in R. Phillips and J. Furlong (eds) *Education, Reform and the State: Twenty-five Years of Politics, Policy and Practice*. London: Routledge-Falmer.

Broadfoot, P., James, M., McMeeking, S., Nuttall, D. and Stierer, B. (1988) *Records of Achievement: Report of the National Evaluation of Pilot Schemes*. London: HMSO.

Brown, A. (2001) Paradise lost and paradise postponed: vocational education and training policy in Germany and England, *Work, Employment and Society*, 15(2): 403–9.

Brown, P. and Lauder, H. (eds) (1992) *Education for Economic Survival: From Fordism to Post-Fordism?* London: Routledge.

Brown, P. and Lauder, H. (2001) *Capitalism and Social Progress: The Future of Society in a Global Economy*. Basingstoke: Palgrave.

Brown, S., Duffield, J. and Riddell, S. (1993) School effectiveness research: the policy makers' tool for school improvement, *EERA Bulletin*, 1(1): 6–15.

Brown, P., Green, A. and Lauder, H. (2001) *High Skills: Globalisation, Competitiveness and Skill Formation*. Oxford: Oxford University Press.

Bruner, J. (1971) *The Relevance of Education*. London: George Allen & Unwin.

Bullock, K.M. and Fertig, M. (2003) Partners in learning or monitors for attendance? Views on personal tutorials from further education, *Research in Post-Compulsory Education*, 8(2): 279–93.

Bullock, K.M. and Jamieson, I.M. (1995) The effect of personal development planning on attitudes, behaviour and understanding, *Educational Studies*, 21(2): 307–21.

Bullock, K.M. and Wikeley, F.J. (1999) Improving learning in Year 9: making use of personal learning plans, *Educational Studies*, 25(1): 19–33.

Bullock, K.M. and Wikeley, F.J. (2000) Personal learning plans: supporting pupil learning, *Topic*, 24(8): 1–9.

Bullock, K.M. and Wikeley, F.J (2003) Personal learning planning: can tutoring improve pupils' learning?, *Pastoral Care in Education*, 21(1): 18–25.

Bullock, K.M., Bishop, K., Martin, S. and Reid, A. (2002) Learning from coursework in English and Geography, *Cambridge Journal of Education*, 32(3): 325–40.

Bullock, K.M., Harris, A. and Jamieson, I.M. (1996) Personal development plans and equal opportunities, *Educational Research*, 38(1): 21–35.

Burden, R. and Nicholls, L. (2000) Evaluating the process of introducing a thinking skills programme into the secondary school curriculum, *Research Papers in Education*, 15(3): 293–306.

Byrne, B.M. and Shavelson, R.J. (1986) On the structure of adolescent self-concept, *Journal of Educational Psychology*, 78: 474–81.

Callaghan, J. (1976) *Towards a National Debate*, http://education.guardian.co.uk/thegreatdebate/story/.

Carmichael, R., Palermo, J., Reeve, L. and Vallence, K. (2001) Student learning: 'the heart of quality' in education and training, *Assessment & Evaluation in Higher Education*, 26(5): 449–63.

Carnell, E. and Lodge, C. (2002) *Supporting Effective Learning*. London: Paul Chapman.

Clarke, P. (2000) *Learning Schools, Learning Systems*. London: Continuum.

Claxton, G. (1990) *Teaching to Learn*. London: Cassell.

Claxton, G. (ed.) (1996) *Liberating the Learner: Lessons for Professional Development in Education*. London: Routledge.

Connexions (2001) http://www.dfes.gov.uk/index.htm.

Cooper, P. and McIntyre, D. (1996) *Effective Teaching and Learning: Teachers' and Students' Perspectives*. Buckingham: Open University Press.

Creemers, B. (1994) *The Effective Classroom*. London: Cassell.

Daniels, H. (ed.) (1996) *An Introduction to Vygotsky*. London: Routledge.

Davies, P. (2001) *Closing the Achievement Gap: Colleges Making a Difference*. London: LSDA.

Dearing, R. (1994) *The National Curriculum and its Assessment: Final Report*. London: School Curriculum and Assessment Authority.

Dearing, R. (1995) *Looking Forward: Careers Education and Guidance in the Curriculum*. London: School Curriculum and Assessment Authority.

Dearing, R. (1996) *Review of Qualifications for 16–19 Year Olds*. London: Department for Education and Employment.

Dearing, R. (1997) *The National Committee of Inquiry into Higher Education*. London: Department for Education and Employment.

Department for Education and Employment (1998) *Target Setting in Schools, Circular 11/98*. London: Department for Education and Employment.

Department for Education and Employment (1999) *All Our Futures: Creativity, Culture and Education*, report of the National Advisory Committee on Creative and Cultural Education. London: Department for Education and Employment.

Department for Education and Skills (2000) *Citizenship: The National Curriculum for England Key Stages 3–4*. London: HMSO.

Department for Education and Skills (2001) *Schools Achieving Success*. London: HMSO.

Department for Education and Skills (2002) *Education and Skills: Delivering Results. A Strategy to 2006*. London: Department for Education and Skills.

Dewey, J. (1956) *The Child and the Curriculum: The School and Society*. Chicago: University of Chicago Press.

Dimmock, C. and Walker, A. (2000) Globalisation and societal culture: redefining schooling and school leadership in the twenty–first century, *Compare*, 30(3): 303–12.

Drummond, M.J. (2001) Children yesterday, today and tomorrow, in J. Collins and D. Cook (eds) *Understanding Learning: Influences and Outcomes*. London: Paul Chapman Publishing.

Dryden, G. and Vos, J. (1994) *The Learning Revolution: A Lifelong Learning Programme for the World's Finest Computer: Your Amazing Brain*. Aylesbury: Accelerated Learning.

Duffield, J., Allen, J., Turner, E. and Morris, B. (2000) Pupils' voices on achievement: an alternative to the standards agenda, *Cambridge Journal of Education*, 30(2): 263–73.

Duffy, A. and Duffy, T. (2002) Psychometric properties of Honey and Mumford's Learning Styles Questionnaire (LSQ), *Personality and Individual Differences*, 33(1): 147–63.

Dweck, C. (2000) *Self-theories: Their Role in Motivation, Personality and Development*. Hove: Psychology Press.

Earl, L., Watson, N., Levin, B., Fullan, M. and Torrance, N. (2003) *Watching & Learning 3: Final Report of the External Evaluation of England's National Literacy and Numeracy Strategies.* Nottingham: DfES.

Education Queensland (2001) http://education.qld.gov.au/public_media/reports/curriculum-framework/.

Edwards, D. and Mercer, N. (1987) *Common Knowledge the Development of Understanding in the Classroom.* London: Methuen.

Edwards, R. (2001) Meeting individual learner needs: power, subject, subjection, in C. Praechter, M. Preedy, D. Scott and J. Soler (eds) *Knowledge, Power and Learning.* London: Paul Chapman Publishing.

Elliott, J. (1996) School effectiveness research and its critics: alternative visions of schooling, *Cambridge Journal of Education,* 26(2): 199–223.

Elliott, J. (2000) Towards a synoptic vision of educational change, in H. Altrichter and J. Elliott (eds) *Images of Educational Change.* Buckingham: Open University Press.

Elwood, J. (1995) Undermining gender stereotypes: examination and coursework performance in the UK at 16, *Assessment in Education,* 2(3): 283–303.

Entwhistle, N. (1981) *Styles of Learning and Teaching.* London: Wiley.

Entwistle, N. and Smith, C. (2002) Personal understanding and target understanding: mapping influences on the outcomes of learning, *British Journal of Educational Psychology,* 72: 321–42.

Fielding, M. (1997) Beyond school effectiveness and school improvement: lighting the slow fuse of possibility, *The Curriculum Journal,* 8(1): 7–27.

Fielding, M. (2001) Beyond the rhetoric of student voice: new departures or new constraints in the transformation of 21st century schooling? *Forum,* 43(2): 100–9.

Fitz-gibbon, C. (1993) Evaluation, monitoring and school improvement, *Evaluation and Research in Education,* 7(2): 83–92.

Flecknoe, M. (2001) Target setting: will it help to raise achievement?, *Educational Management and Administration,* 29(2): 217–28.

Fouzder, N. and Markwick, A. (2000) Self-perception, individual learning style and academic achievement by a pair of bilingual twins in secondary school, *International Journal of Science Education,* 22(6): 583–601.

Fullan, M. (1991) *The New Meaning of Educational Change.* London: Cassell.

Fullan, M. (1993) *Change Forces: Probing the Depths of Educational Reform.* London: Falmer Press.

Gage, N.L. and Berliner, D.C. (1984) *Educational Psychology.* Boston, MA: Houghton Mifflin.

Gagné, R. (1975) *Essentials of Learning for Instruction.* Chicago: Dryden.

Gardner, H. (1993) *Multiple Intelligences: The Theory in Practice.* New York: Basic Books.

Garner, I. (2000) Problems and inconsistencies with Kolb's learning styles, *Educational Psychology,* 20(3): 341–8.

Gipps, C. (1994) *Beyond Testing: Towards a Theory of Educational Assessment*. London: Falmer Press.

Graham, S. and Weiner, B. (1996) Theories and principles of motivation, in D.C. Berliner and R.C. Calfee (eds) *Handbook of Educational Psychology*. New York: Simon & Schuster.

Gray, J. (1995) The quality of schooling: frameworks for judgement, in J. Gray and B. Wilcox (eds) *Good School, Bad School*. Buckingham: Open University Press.

Gray, J. and Wilcox, B. (eds) (1995) *Good School, Bad School*. Buckingham: Open University Press.

Gray, J., Goldstein, H. and Thomas, S. (2003) Of trends and trajectories: searching for patterns in school improvement, *British Educational Research Journal*, 29(1): 83–8.

Green, M. (2002) *Improving One-one Tutorials*. London: Learning and Skills Development Agency.

Handy, C. (1997) Schools for life and work, in P. Mortimore and V. Little (eds) *Living Education: Essays in Honour of John Tomlinson*. London: Paul Chapman.

Hargreaves, A. (ed.) (1998) *International Handbook of Educational Change*. London: Kluwer.

Hargreaves, D. (1999) Helping practitioners explore their school's culture, in. J. Prosser (ed.) *School Culture*. London: Paul Chapman.

Hargreaves, D. (2001) A new theory of school effectiveness and improvement, *British Educational Research Journal*, 27(4): 487–504.

Hargreaves, D., Molly, C. and Pratt, A. (1982) Social factors in conservation, *British Journal of Psychology*, 73: 231–4.

Harris, A., Jamieson, I. and Russ, J. (1995) A study of effective departments in secondary schools, *School Organisation*, 15(3): 283–99.

Harris, D. and Bell, C. (1986) *Evaluating and Assessing in Learning*. London: Kogan Page.

Hayes, D. (2001) Impact of mentoring on student primary teachers, *Mentoring and Tutoring*, 9(1): 5–21.

Henson, R.K. and Hwang, D. (2002) Variability and prediction of measurement error in Kolb's Learning Style Inventory scores: a reliability generalization study, *Educational and Psychological Measurement*, 62: 712.

Hidi, S. (2003) Emotional and cognitive aspects of motivation. Paper delivered at the EARLI Conference, Padua, Italy August 26–30.

Hodkinson, P. and Sparkes, A. (1993) To tell or not to tell? Reflecting on ethical dilemmas in stakeholder research, *Evaluation and Research in Education*, 7(3): 117–32.

Hofstede, G.H. (1991) *Cultures and Organizations: Software of the Mind*. London: McGraw-Hill.

Holt, G., Boyd, S., Dickinson, B., Loose, J. and O'Donnell, S. (1999) *Education in England, Wales and Northern Ireland: A Guide to the System*. Slough: NFER.

Honey, P. and Mumford, A. (1992) *The Manual of Learning Styles*. Maidenhead: Honey.

Hopkins, D., Ainscow, M. and West, M. (1994) *School Improvement in an Era of Change*. London: Cassell.

Howieson, C. and Semple, S. (1998) The teacher's experience of guidance, in R. Edwards, R. Harrison and A. Tait (eds) *Telling Tales: Perspectives on Guidance and Counselling for Learning*. Buckingham: Open University Press.

International Baccalaureate Organization (2002) *Articulation of the Primary Years Programme, the Middle Years Programme and the Diploma Programme: Monograph*. Geneva: IBO.

International Baccalaureate Organization (2003) *Theory of Knowledge Subject Guide*. Geneva: IBO.

Investors in People (2001) *Investors in People*, http://www.iipuk.co.uk/.

James, M. and Gipps, C. (1998) Broadening the basis of assessment to prevent the narrowing of learning, *The Curriculum Journal*, 9(3): 285–97.

Jamieson, I. and Wikeley, F. (2000) 'Is consistency a necessary characteristic for effective schools? *School Effectiveness and School Improvement*, 21(4): 435–53.

Jamieson, I. and Wikeley, F. (2001) A contextual perspective: fitting school round the needs of students, in N. Bennett and A. Harris (eds) *School Effectiveness and School Improvement: Perspectives on an Elusive Partnership*. London: Cassell.

Jonassen, D.H. and Grabowski, B.L. (1993) *Handbook of Individual Differences Learning and Instruction*. Hillsdale, NJ: Lawrence Erlbaum Associates.

Joyce, B., Calhoun, E and Hopkins, D. (1997) *Models of Learning – Tools for Teaching*. Buckingham: Open University Press.

Kaplan, A. (1997) Work, leisure, and the tasks of schooling, *Curriculum Inquiry*, 27(4): 423–51.

Kelly, A.V. (1999) *The Curriculum: Theory and Practice*, 4th edn. London: Sage.

Killeen, J. (1996) The social context of guidance, in A. Watts, B. Law, J. Killeen, J. Kidd and R. Hawthorn (eds) *Rethinking Careers Education and Guidance: Theory, Policy and Practice*. London: Routledge.

Klein, P.D. (2003) Rethinking the multiplicity of cognitive resources and curricular representations: alternatives to 'learning styles' and 'multiple intelligences', *Journal of Curriculum Studies*, 35(1): 45–81.

Koh, A. (2000) Linking learning, knowledge creation and business creativity: a preliminary assessment of the East Asian quest for creativity, *Technological Forecasting and Social Change*, 64: 85–100.

Kolb, D. (1984) *Experiential Learning: Experience as a Source of Learning and Development*. Englewood Cliffs, NJ: Prentice Hall.

Kress, G. (2000) A curriculum for the future, *Cambridge Journal of Education*, 30(1): 133–45.

Kumar, K. (1997) The post-modern condition, in A.H. Halsey, H. Lauder, P. Brown and A.S. Wells (eds) *Education: Culture, Economy and Society*. Oxford: Oxford University Press.

Kyriacou, C. (1992) *Effective Teaching in Schools*. London: Simon & Schuster.

Lang, P. and Marland, M. (1985) *New Directions in Pastoral Care*. Oxford: Blackwell.

Lauder, H., Jamieson, I. and Wikeley, F. (1998) Models of school effectiveness: limits and capabilities, in R. Slee, G. Weiner and S. Tomlinson (eds) *School Effectiveness for Whom? Challenges to the School Effectiveness and School Improvement Movements*. London: Falmer Press.

Lave, J. and Wenger, E. (1991) *Situated Learning: Legitimate Peripheral Participation*. Cambridge: Cambridge University Press.

Lawton, D. (1973) *Social Change, Educational Theory and Curriculum Planning*. London: Hodder & Stoughton.

Lawton, D. (1996) *Beyond the National Curriculum*. London: Hodder & Stoughton.

Levacic, R. and Woods, P. (2002) Raising school performance in the league tables (Part 1): disentangling the effects of social disadvantage, *British Educational Research Journal*, 28(2): 207–26.

Lim, T.K. (1998) Ascertaining the critical thinking and formal reasoning skills of students, *Research in Education*, 59: 9–18.

Loyten, H. and de Jong, R. (1998) Parallel classes: differences and similarities. Teacher effects and school effects in secondary schools, *School Effectiveness and School Improvement*, 9(4): 437–473.

Lunzer, E. (1989) Cognitive development: learning and the mechanisms of change, in B. Moon and P. Murphy (eds) *Developments in Assessment and Learning*. London: Hodder & Stoughton.

MacBeath, J. (1997) Unlock the secrets of the thinking brain, *Times Educational Supplement*, 20 June: 22.

MacBeath, J., Boyd, B., Rand, J. and Bell, S. (1996) *Schools Speak for Themselves*. London: National Union of Teachers.

MacGilchrist, B., Myers, K. and Reed, J. (1997) *The Intelligent School*. London: Paul Chapman.

Main, A. (1980) *Encouraging Effective Learning*. Edinburgh: Scottish Academic Press.

Marland, M. and Rogers, R. (1997) *The Art of the Tutor: Developing Your Role in the Secondary School*. London: David Fulton.

Marsh, C. (1997) *Key Concepts for Understanding Curriculum*. London: Falmer Press.

Martin, S., Reid, A., Bullock, K. and Bishop, K. (2002) *Voices and Choices in Coursework*. Sheffield: The Geographical Association.

Martinez, P. (2001a) *College Improvement: The Voice of Teachers and Managers*. London: Learning and Skills Development Agency.

Martinez, P. (2001b) *Improving Student Retention and Achievement: What Do We Need to Know and What Do We Need to Find Out?*, London: Learning and Skills Development Agency.

Martinez, P. (2001c) *Great Expectations: Setting Targets for Students*. London: Learning and Skills Development Agency.

Marton, F. and Säljö, R. (1976) On qualitative differences in learning: 1–outcome and process, *British Journal of Educational Psychology*, 46: 4–11.

Maslow, A. (1970) *Motivation and Personality*. London: Harper & Row.

McCarty, C. (2001) http://www.ed.gov/pubs/Research5/UnitedStates/standards.html.

McClune, B. (2001) Modular A-levels – who are the winners and losers? A comparison of lower-sixth and upper-sixth students' performance in linear and modular A-level examinations', *Educational Research*, 43(1): 79–89.

McGuiness, J. (1989) *A Whole School Approach to Pastoral Care*. London: Kogan Page.

McPherson, A. (1993) Measuring added value in schools, in *Briefings for the National Commission on Education*. London: Heinemann.

Miller, A. (1993) *Building Effective School-Business Links*. London: Westex Publications Centre.

Moore, A. (2000) *Teaching and Learning: Pedagogy, Curriculum and Culture*. London: RoutledgeFalmer.

Moore, R. (2000) For knowledge: tradition, progressivism and progress in education – reconstructing the curriculum debate, *Cambridge Journal of Education*, 30(1): 17–36.

Moore, R. and Young, M. (2001) Knowledge and the curriculum in the sociology of education: towards a reconceptualisation, *British Journal of Sociology of Education*, 22(4): 445–61.

Morehouse, R. (1997) Critical thinking and the culture of the school, *Curriculum*, 18(3): 162–70.

Morgan, C. and Morris, G. (1999) *Good Teaching and Learning: Pupils and Teachers Speak*. Buckingham: Open University Press.

Morgan, N. and Saxton, J. (1991) *Teaching, Questioning and Learning*. London: Routledge.

Morrison, H., Cowan, P. and D'Arcy, J. (2001) How defensible are current trends in GCSE mathematics to replace teacher-assessed coursework by examinations?, *Evaluation and Research in Education*, 15(1): 33–50.

Murphy, P.F. (1996) Defining pedagogy, in P.F. Murphy and C.V. Gipps (eds) *Equity in the Classroom*. London: Falmer Press.

Muschamp, Y.M. and Bullock, K.M. (2003) Pupil responsibility in the primary school. Paper presented to the ECER Conference, Hamburg, 2003.

Nisbet, J. and Shucksmith, J. (1986) *Learning Strategies*. London: Routledge & Kegan Paul.

Norman, K. (1992) *Thinking Voices*. London: NCC Enterprises Ltd.

Norwich, B. (1999) Pupils' reasons for learning and behaving and for not learning and behaving in English and Maths lessons in a secondary school, *British Journal of Educational Psychology*, 69: 547–69.

Ofsted (Office for Standards in Education) (1996) *Target Setting to Raise Standards: A Survey of Good Practice*. London: DfEE.

Organization for Economic Cooperation and Development (1996) *Report on Korea*. Seoul: Korean Educational Development Institute.

Organization for Economic Cooperation and Development (2001) *Knowledge and Skills for Life: First Results from the Programme for International Student Assessment*. Paris: OECD.

Owen, J.R. and Rogers, P.J. (1999) *Program Evaluation: Forms and Approaches*. London: Sage.

Palmer, J. (2001) Student drop-out: a case study in new managerialist policy, *Journal of Further and Higher Education*, 25(3): 349–57.

Pavlov, I.P. (1928) *Lectures on Conditioned Reflexes*. New York: Liveright.

Philip, K. and Hendry, L.B. (2000) Making sense of mentoring or mentoring making sense? Reflections on the mentoring process by adult mentors with young people, *Journal of Community & Applied Social Psychology*, 10: 211–23.

Piaget, J. (1971) The stages of intellectual development of the child, in H. Munsinger (ed.) *Readings in Child Development*. New York: Holt, Rinehart & Winston.

Plowden, M. (1967) *Children and their Primary Schools: A Report of the Central Advisory Council for Education (England)*. London: HMSO.

Pole, C.J. (1993) *Assessing and Recording Achievement*. Buckingham: Open University Press.

Pope, N. (2001) An examination of the use of peer rating for formative assessment in the context of the theory of consumption values, *Assessment & Evaluation in Higher Education*, 26(3): 235–46.

Praechter, C. (2001) Power, gender and curriculum, in C. Praechter, M. Preedy, D. Scott and J. Soler (eds) *Knowledge, Power and Learning*. London: Paul Chapman.

Quality Assurance Agency (2001) *Guidelines on HE Progress File*. London: QAA.

QCA (2003) National Qualifications Framework http://www.qca.org.uk/nq/framework

Raffo, C. (2003) Disaffected young people and the work-related curriculum at Key Stage 4: issues of social capital development and learning as a form of cultural practice, *Journal of Education and Work*, 16(1): 69–86.

Reynolds, D. (1997) East-west trade-off, *Times Educational Supplement*, 27 June: 21.

Reynolds, D. and Farrell, S. (1996) *Worlds Apart? A Review of International Surveys of Educational Achievement Including England*. London: HMSO.

Reynolds, D., Sammons, P., Stoll, L., Barber, M. and Hillman, J. (1996) School effectiveness and school improvement in the United Kingdom, *School Effectiveness and School Improvement*, 7(2): 134–53.

Riding, R.J. and Rayner, S. (1998) *Cognitive styles and Learning Strategies*. London: David Fulton.

Riding, R.J. and Read, G. (1996) Cognitive styles and pupil preferences, *Educational Psychology*, 16(1): 81–105.

Riley, K. and Nuttall, D. (eds) (1994) *Measuring Quality*. London: Falmer Press.

Roberts, E. and Miller, A. (1991) *School-Based Industry Coordinator Professional Development Activities*. Warwick: University of Warwick Centre for Education and Industry.

Rogers, P. (1990) Discovery, learning, critical thinking and the nature of knowledge, *British Journal of Educational Studies*, 28(1): 3–14.

Rowntree, D. (1974) *Educational Technology in Curriculum Development*. London: Harper & Row.

Rowntree, D. (1988) The side-effects of assessment, in R. Dale, R. Fergusson and A. Robinson (eds) *Frameworks for Teaching*. London: Hodder & Stoughton.

Rudduck, J., Chaplain, R. and Wallace, G. (1996) *School Improvement: What Can Pupils Tell Us?* London: Fulton.

Russian Federation (1996) *Russia's Educational System: National Report of the Russian Federation*. Moscow: Ministry of Education (presented at the 45th session of the International Conference on Education, Geneva 1996).

Sadler-Smith, E. (2001) A reply to Reynolds's critique of learning style, *Management Learning*, 32(3): 291–304.

Sammons, P. and Reynolds, D. (1997) A partisan evaluation – John Elliott on school effectiveness, *Cambridge Journal of Education*, 27(1): 123–36.

Sammons, P., Thomas, S. and Mortimore, P. (1997) *Forging Links: Effective Schools and Effective Departments*. London: Paul Chapman.

Schagen, I. (1995) *Quantitative Analysis for Self- Evaluation*. Slough: National Foundation for Educational Research.

Schagen, I. and Morrison, J. (1999) A methodology for judging departmental performance within schools, *Educational Research*, 41(1): 3–10.

Schön, D. (1983) *The Reflective Practitioner: How Professionals Think in Action*. London: Temple Smith.

Schostak, J. (2000) Developing under developing circumstances: the personal and social development of students and the process of schooling, in H. Altrichter and J. Elliott (eds) *Images of Educational Change*. Buckingham: Open University Press.

Scottish Office Education and Industry Department (SOEID) (1996) *How Good is Our School?* London: HMI.

SCRE (2001) *Thinking Skills*, http://www.scre.ac.uk/scot-research/thinking/.

Shen, C. and Pedulla, J.J. (2000) The relationship between students' achievements and their self-perception of competence and rigour in mathematics and science: a cross-national analysis, *Assessment in Education*, 7(2): 237–53.

Simkins, T. and Lumby, J. (2002) Cultural transformation in further education? Mapping the debate, *Research in Post-Compulsory Education*, 7(1): 9–25.

Skinner, B.F. (1938) *The Behaviour of Organisms*. New York: Appleton-Century-Crofts.

Smith, A. (1998) *Accelerated Learning*. Stafford: Network Educational Press.

Stenhouse, L. (1975) *An Introduction to Curriculum Research and Development*. London: Heinemann.

Sternberg, R.J. (1989) Second game: a school's-eye view of intelligence, in B. Moon and P. Murphy (eds) *Developments in Learning and Assessment*. London: Hodder & Stoughton.

Sternberg, R.J. and Lubart, T.I. (1992) Creativity: its nature and assessment, *School Psychology International*, 13(3): 243–53.

Stoll, L. and Fink, D. (1996) *Changing Our Schools*. Buckinghamshire: Open University Press.

Swailes, S. and Senior, B. (1999) The dimensionality of Honey and Mumford's Learning Styles Questionnaire, *International Journal of Selection and Assessment*, 7(1): 1–11.

Teacher Training Agency (2002) *Qualifying to Teach: Professional Standards for Qualified Teacher Status and Requirements for Initial Teacher Training*. London: DfES.

Technical and Vocational Education Initiative (1991) *Flexible Learning: A Framework for Education and Training in the Skills Decade*. Sheffield: The Employment Department.

Thomas, G. and McRobbie, C. (1999) Using metaphor to probe students' conceptions of chemistry learning, *International Journal of Science Education*, 21(6): 667–85.

Thrupp, M. (1997) How school mix shapes school processes: a comparative study of New Zealand schools, *New Zealand Journal of Educational Studies*, 32(1): 53–81.

Tomlinson, P. and Kilmer, S. (1991) *Flexible Learning, Flexible Teaching: The Flexible Learning Framework and Current Educational Theory*. Sheffield: The Employment Department.

Tomlinson, J. and Little, V. (2000) Educated for the 21st century, *Children and Society*, 14: 243–53.

Topping, K.J. (1998) Peer assessment between students in college and university, *Review of Educational Research*, 68(3): 249–67.

Vygotsky , L.S. (1978) *Mind in Society: The Development of Higher Psychological Processes*. Cambridge, MA: Harvard University Press.

Vygotsky, L.S. (1986) *Thought and Language*. Cambridge MA: MIT Press.

Wallace, B. (ed.) (2001) *Teaching Skills Across the Primary Curriculum*. London: David Fulton/NACE.

Wallace, M. and Poulson, L. (2003) *Learning to Read Critically in Educational Management*. London: Sage.

Waterhouse, P. (1990) *Flexible Learning: An Outline*. Bath: Network Educational Press.

Watts, A. (1992) Individual action planning: issues and strategies, *British Journal of Education and Work*, 5(1): 47–64.

Watts, A. (1993) Promoting careers: guidance for learning and work, in National Commission on Education, *Briefings*. London: Heinemann.

Welsh Joint Education Committee (2002) *The Welsh Baccalaureate Qualification*. Cardiff: WJEC.

Welsh Baccalaureate Qualification (2003) *Job Description of the WBQ Personal Tutor*. Cardiff: WBQ.

Wheldall, K. and Glynn, T. (1989) *Effective Classroom Learning: A Behaviourist Interactionist Approach to Teaching*. Oxford: Basil Blackwell.

Wikeley, F. (2000) Researchers feeding back to teachers, in S. Askew (ed.) *Feedback for Learning*. London: Routledge.

Wikeley, F. and Stables, A. (1999) Changes in school students' approaches to subject option choices: a longitudinal study in the West of England, *Educational Research*, 41(3): 287–301.

Wildy, H. and Wallace, J. (1998) Professionalism, portfolios and the development of school leaders, *School Leadership and Management*, 18(1): 123–40.

Williams, S. (1999) Policy tensions in vocational education and training for young people: the origins of General National Vocational Qualifications, *Journal of Education Policy*, 14(2): 151–66.

Willis, P. (1990) *Common Culture: Symbolic Work at Play in the Everyday Culture of the Young*. Buckingham: Open University Press.

Wood, D. (1998) *How Children Think and Learn*. Oxford: Blackwell.

Woods, P. and Levacic, R. (2002) Raising school performance in the league tables (Part 2): barriers to responsiveness in three disadvantaged schools, *British Educational Research Journal*, 28(2): 227–48.

Wragg, E.C., Wikeley, F.J., Wragg, C.M. and Haynes, G.S. (1996) *Teacher Appraisal Observed*. London: Routledge.

Young, M. (2003) *Curriculum Studies and the Problem of Knowledge: Updating the Enlightenment*. Paper presented at University of Bath to an internal seminar.

Index

Abbott, J. 61, 127
academic knowledge 93–4
academic self-concept 34–5
access to tutorial file 86
accountability 3–4, 105
action planning 9, 81–9
    follow up 86–8
    recording the plan 57–8, 84–6,
    125–6
    sharing the plan with subject
    teachers 114–15
    target setting 81–4
adult (ego state) 125
Angier, C. 122
Argyris, C. 73
arts 118
assessment 9, 104–5
    formative 79–80, 104–5
    and National Curriculum
    104–5, 107–8
attainment 127
    impact on learning 69–70, 75
    testing 107–8
attitude to change 123
audio recording 125–6
Australia 98
Ausubel, D. 64, 66
autonomous learning 4–6

Bailin, S. 39
Bandura, A. 34
Barber, M. 102

baseline testing 108
behaviour 100
behaviourist approaches to
    learning 62–3
Bell, C. 36, 70
belonging, sense of 127
Beltman, S. 126
benchmarking 7
Benson, P. 66
Berne, E. 124–5
Bernstein, B. 69
Biggs, J.B. 123
Bishop, K.N. 61, 80, 93, 96, 104
Black, P. 104, 105
Blair, T. 11
Bloom, B.S. 65
Bornholt, L.J. 34
Boud, D. 38, 39, 72, 73
Bourdieu, P. 44
boys 69–70, 127
Broadfoot, P. 14, 73, 84, 105
Brown, P. 4, 8
Bruner, J. 10, 65, 70
Bullock, K.M. 20, 24, 26–7, 38,
    40, 43, 45, 54, 57, 66, 72, 84,
    86, 96, 100, 110, 113, 123, 124
Burden, R. 109
Byrne, B.M. 34

career planning 9, 14, 110–12
Careers Service 14, 16, 110
Carnell, E. 31

challenging feedback 54
change, attitude to 123
child (ego state) 125
child development, stages in 63–4
choices for learning 109–15
  between subjects 109–13
  sharing choices 114–15
  within subjects 113–14
citizenship education 94–5
Clarke, P. 90, 96
Claxton, G. 36, 71, 72
Cognitive Abilities Test (CAT)
  scores 82
cognitive styles 66–9
cognitive theory 63–4
common practices 123
communication
  between students, tutors and
  subject teachers 114–15
  educational relationships and
  124–6
community involvement 95
compulsory education 90
concepts 65
concrete operations stage 64
confidentiality 115
Connexions Service 16–19
content of curriculum 97–102
contested curriculum 115–18
context for learning 3–4
continuing professional
  development 26–7
continuity 25
Cooper, P. 74
counselling 36
  skills 54
coursework 66, 113–14
creative and cultural education 9
creativity 4–6
criteria, understanding 40–1
critical thinking 38–41, 65, 80–1
cultural capital 43–4, 121
culture, school 122–4

curriculum 2, 10, 90–106
  assessment and standards
  104–5
  content 97–102
  contested 115–18
  dilemmas 91–2
  purposes of 92–7
  supporting students in
  107–19
  choices for learning 109–15
  for 21st century 95–7
  who determines the curriculum
  102–4

Daniels, H. 30
Davies, P. 15, 31
Dearing, R. 14, 99
Department for Education and
  Employment 9, 14
Department for Education and
  Skills 92, 94, 95, 99, 100, 101,
  104
  citizenship education 95
Dewey, J. 65, 91
dialogue *see* one-to-one dialogue
Dimmock, C. 122
double loop learning 73
Drummond, M.J. 116
Dweck, C. 72

Earl, L. 99
early years curriculum 116–17
economic performativity 92
Education Act 1999 92
education policy 3–4
Education Queensland 98
Education Reform Act 1988 98,
  107
educational ideology 12
educational initiatives 5, 14
educational relationships 20,
  43–4, 120–8
  and communication 124–6

as motivators 126–7
power in 27–30, 38, 51, 55, 86, 124
and school culture 122–4
Edwards, D. 12
Edwards, R. 124, 125
effort 7–8
ego states 124–5
Elliott, J. 92
emotional intelligence 72, 75
employment opportunities 93, 109
empowerment 9
Entwistle, N. 12
espoused theories 72–3
evaluation 38–41
evidence, gathering 39
examinations 104, 126
expectations, institutional 123
experiential learning 67
extracurricular activities 100
extrinsic motivation 126

facts, theories and skills *see* curriculum
feedback 36–7, 51–5, 79–80
Fertig, M. 24, 26–7
Fielding, M. 38, 123
Flecknoe, M. 82, 87
Flexible Learning Project 14
follow up 86–8
formal logical operations stage 64
formative assessment 79–80, 104–5
frameworks 5, 65
further education colleges 15
see also institutions
Further Education Funding Council 90

Gagné, R. 63, 65
Gardner, H. 60
gender 69–70, 75

General Certificate of Secondary Education (GCSE) 5, 61
genuine dialogue 49–55
'getting to know you' tutors 47–8
Gipps, C. 104, 105
globalization 92
Goleman, D. 73, 74
good practice, sharing 7
Grabowski, B.L. 67
Graham, S. 72
Gray, J. 27, 42
Green, M. 26
group discussions 30, 78
small-group discussions 20, 30, 41, 56–7, 78
whole-group sessions 24, 29–30

Handy, C. 60
Hargreaves, D. 96, 100, 105
Harris, D. 36, 70
Hayes, D. 37
Hendry, L.B. 121
hidden curriculum 100
Hidi, S. 115
hierarchy of needs 127
higher-level skills 4–6, 65
history 118
Hodkinson, P. 25, 99
Hofstede, G. 122
honest feedback 54–5
Honey, P. 67
Howieson, C. 20

ice-breaking activities 28
ideology, educational 12
individual career planning 9, 14
individual learning discussion *see* one-to-one dialogue
information processing
learning as 64–5
skills 78–81

institutions
  culture 122–4
  expectations 123
  issues and personal tutoring
    21–30
  target setting 81–3
intelligence 60–1
  emotional 72, 75
interconnected curriculum 96
International Baccalaureate 95–6,
  101
  Theory of Knowledge 117–18
intrinsic motivation 51, 126
Investors in People standard 15
Italy 116–17

Jonassen, D.H. 66
Joyce, B. 69
'jumping through hoops' tutors
  46–7

Kelly, A.V. 91, 97, 98, 107
key skills 99–102
Key Skills Qualifications 101
key stage specialization 25
Killeen, J. 96
Klein, P.D. 68
Kolb, D. 67, 68
Kress, G. 91, 96
Kyriacou, C. 61

large group sessions 30
Lauder, H. 4, 8
Lave, J. 65, 69
Lawton, D. 91, 97, 98, 102
learning
  definitions 61
  individuals and 2, 120
  lifelong 3, 4–6, 32
  setting targets and 83–4
  social dimension of 74, 75, 77
  theories of 62–6
learning cycle 67, 68

learning process model 61–2
learning skills/techniques 2, 10,
  35, 60–75
  centrality of reflection 72–4
  helping students develop
    76–89
    follow up 86–8
    information gathering and
      processing 78–81
    recording the action plan
      84–6
    setting targets and objectives
      81–4
  higher-level skills 4–6, 65
  learning styles 66–70
  motivations for learning 71–2
  talking about learning 70–1
learning society 3, 4
learning styles 66–70
Learning Styles Inventory 67
lifelong learning 3, 4–6, 32
Little, V. 92
Lodge, C. 31
long–term planning 110–12
Lubart, T.I. 104, 126
Lumby, J. 31
Lunzer, E. 64

MacBeath, J. 4, 36
MacGilchrist, B. 6, 21, 120
management 7
Marsh, C. 97, 100, 102
Martin, S. 5, 40, 65
Martinez, P. 15, 82, 86
Marton, F. 65
Maslow, A. 127
mathematics 117
McCarty, C. 98
McGuinness, J. 13
McIntyre, D. 74
McRobbie, C. 32, 37
measurement 3–4
mentoring 55, 121

Mercer, N. 12
Mini–enterprise in Schools
    Project 5
mixed ability groups 77
modularization 9
Moore, A. 123
Moore, P.J. 123
Moore, R. 91, 100, 102, 103, 108
morality 101
'more capable others' 121
Morehouse, R. 41
Morgan, C. 66, 70, 88, 103
Morgan, N. 81
Morris, G. 66, 70, 88, 103
motivation 9, 51, 71–2, 93, 112
    educational relationships as
    motivators 126–7
Mumford, A. 67
Muschamp, Y.M. 110

National Advisory Committee on
    Creative and Cultural
    Education 9
national culture 122
National Curriculum 4, 12,
    98–101
    and assessment 104–5, 107–8
National Literacy Strategy 99
National Numeracy Strategy 99
natural sciences 118
needs, hierarchy of 127
negative strokes 125
neuro-linguistic programming
    (NLP) 68
Nichols, L. 109
Nisbet, J. 60
Norman, K. 38, 71
note-taking 125

one-to-one dialogue 9–10, 10–11,
    20, 71, 75
    establishing a genuine dialogue
    49–55

preparation for 55–7
recording 27–8, 57–8, 84–6,
    125–6
student ownership/control
    27–8, 29–30, 38, 51, 86
student self–knowledge 35–8
tutorial provision 24
Organization for Economic
    Cooperation and
    Development 1
organizational culture 122–4
outcomes 46–7
    compulsion for 45–6
ownership, student 27–30, 38, 51,
    85–6

Palmer, J. 38
parent (ego state) 124
Passeron, J.C. 44
pastoral care 13–14
Pavlov, I.P. 63
Pedulla, J.J. 34
peer group dynamics 126–7
performance data 39, 81–2
personal development 13–14
Personal Learning Planning (PLP)
    9, 17–19, 20, 110–13
personal reflection see
    reflection
personal, social and health
    education 100
personal tutoring 1, 2, 12–31
    Connexions Service 16–19
    embedding in school culture
    123–4
    further education colleges 15
    institutional issues 21–30
    moving towards 8–10
    need for 13–15
    tutorial programme 24, 29–30
    tutors, students and
    educational relationships 20
    Welsh Baccalaureate 15–16

Philip, K. 121
Piaget, J. 63–4
planning 14–15
    action planning *see* action
    planning
    career planning 9, 14, 110–12
    long-term planning 110–12
    Personal Learning Planning 9,
    17–19, 20, 110–13
policy context 3–4
political literacy 95
portfolios 9
positive feedback 53–4
positive strokes 125
post-compulsory education 3, 90
Poulson, L. 39
Povey, H. 122
power, in educational relationship
    27–30, 38, 51, 55, 86, 124
power distance 123
practical skills 93
Praechter, C. 123
pre-operational period 63
preparation for dialogue 55–7
prescribed curriculum 12
    see also National Curriculum
professional development 25,
    26–7
Progress File 17
purpose of curriculum 92–6
    students' understanding of
    96–7

qualifications 93–4, 100–2, 104–5,
    108
    *see also under individual
    qualifications*
qualitative data 55
quantitative data 55

Rayner, S. 66, 67
Read, G. 67, 104
reading 53

recording dialogue 27–8, 57–8,
    84–6, 125–6
Records of Achievement 9, 14, 17
reflection 56, 126
    self-knowledge 35–8
    and skills for learning 72–4,
    80
reflective cycle 73–4
'reflective tutors' 49
Reggio-Emilia, Italy 116–17
relationships, educational *see*
    educational relationships
review 87–9, 123–4
Reynolds, D. 4, 6
Riding, R.J. 67, 68, 104
Robinson, F. 64, 66
routines 97
Rowntree, D. 63
Rudduck, J. 36, 70, 72, 86
Rudolf Steiner schools 116–17
Russian Federation 94

Sadler-Smith, E. 67
Säljö, R. 65
Sammons, P. 6
Saxton, J. 81
scaffolding 65
Schön, D. 72, 73
school improvement 6–8
schools
    culture 122–4
    target setting 81–4
    see also institutions
Schools Curriculum and
    Assessment Authority (SCAA),
    *Desirable Outcomes for Children's
    Learning on Entering Compulsory
    Education* 116–17
Schostak, J. 102
self-assessment 38–41, 56, 79–80
self-concept, academic 34–5
self-efficiency theory 34
self-esteem 9, 127

self-knowledge 2, 10, 32–42
  meaning 33–8
    self-assessment and
    evaluation 38–41
    supporting learners in 43–59
    compulsion for outcomes
    45–6
    genuine dialogue 49–55
    preparation for dialogue
    55–7
    recording dialogue 57–8
    types of tutors 46–9
self-stereotyping 34–5
Semple, S. 20
sensori-motor stage 63
Shavelson, R.J. 34
Shen, C. 34
Shucksmith, J. 60
Simkins, T. 31
single loop learning 73
skilled workforce 3, 4, 92, 93
skills
  learning skills *see* learning
  skills/techniques
  practical 93
  thinking skills 78–80, 100–2
  transdisciplinary 100–1
Skinner, B.F. 63
small-group discussions 20, 30,
  41, 56–7, 77
SMART targets 82–3
Smith, A. 68
Smith, C. 12–13
social constructivist theories of
  learning 64–5, 121
social dimension of learning 74,
  75, 77
social and moral responsibility
  95
Sparkes, A. 25, 99
specific feedback 52–3
Stables, A. 109
staff development 25, 26–7

stages of cognitive development
  63–4
standard assessment tests (SATs)
  107–8
standards 3, 14
  curriculum, assessment and
  104–5
Sternberg, R.J. 60, 61, 70, 104,
  126
stimulus-response (S-R) theories
  62–3
stress 80–1
strokes 125
student-centred learning 7, 12
student-student interactions 41
  see also group discussions
students
  benefits of personal tutoring
  20
  ownership/control 27–30, 38,
  51, 85–6
  preparation for dialogue 56–7
  responsibility for learning
  103
  sharing choices with subject
  teachers 114–15
  understanding of purposes of
  curriculum 97–8
styles, learning 67–70
subject choices 109–13
subject teachers
  communication with students
  and tutors 114–15
  as personal tutors 114
summative assessment 104–5
'super tutors' 22
supporting students
  developing skills for learning
  76–89
  to know themselves 43–59
  in knowing what to learn
  107–19
Swailes, S. 68

talk 70–1
targets
    achieving 86–8
    setting 14, 58, 81–4, 112
Teacher Training Agency,
    *Standards for Qualified Teacher
    Status* 75
teachers
    and content of curriculum
    102–4
    subject teachers 114–15
Technical and Vocational
    Education Initiative 5, 14
technology of instruction 63
testing 82, 107–8
theoretical knowledge 92–3
theories of learning 62–6
theories in use 72
Theory of Knowledge (TOK)
    117–18
thinking skills 78–80, 100–1
Thomas, G. 32, 37
timetabling 21–2
Tomlinson, J. 92
Topping, K.J. 56
transdisciplinary skills 100–1
'transmission' approach 12
tutorial file 86
tutorial programme 24, 29–30
tutors 103
    benefits of personal tutoring
    20
    characteristics of a good tutor
    23
    continuing professional
    development 26–7
    own learning processes 124

preparation for dialogue 55–6
professionalization/status 22, 23
role 37, 44, 115
subject teachers as 114
types of 46–9
see also personal tutoring

United States (US) 98

values, shared 24–5
vocational routes 9, 99
Vygotsky, L.S. 65, 70, 121

Walker, A. 122
Walker, D. 73
Wallace, M. 39
Watts, A. 14, 109
Weiner, B. 72
Welsh Baccalaureate Qualification
    (WBQ) 15–16, 101
Welsh Joint Education Committee
    16
Wenger, E. 65, 69
whole-group sessions 24, 29–30
Wikeley, F. 38, 43, 45, 54, 72, 84,
    86, 100, 109, 123, 124
Wiliam, D. 106
Wood, D. 124
work-related learning programme
    99
workforce, skilled 3, 4, 92, 93
Wragg, E.C. 41

Young, M. 91, 108, 116

zone of proximal development
    (ZPD) 65